Substitutes

On

Union Station

Also by the author in reading order:

Destiny: Union Station
Date Night on Union Station
Alien Night on Union Station
High Priest on Union Station
Spy Night on Union Station
Carnival on Union Station
Wanderers on Union Station
Vacation on Union Station
Guest Night on Union Station
Word Night on Union Station
Party Night on Union Station
Review Night on Union Station
Family Night on Union Station
Book Night on Union Station
LARP Night on Union Station
Career Night on Union Station
Last Night on Union Station
Independent Living
Soup Night on Union Station
Assisted Living
Freelance on the Galactic Tunnel Network
Con Living
Empire Night on Union Station
Space Living
Traders on the Galactic Tunnel Network
Orphans on the Galactic Tunnel Network
Swap Night on Union Station
Slow Living
Artists on the Galactic Tunnel Network
History Night on Union Station
Bits of Anarchy
Double Living
Bits of Flower
Synergy on the Galactic Tunnel Network

Substitutes

On

Union Station

Book Twenty-One of EarthCent Ambassador

Foner Books

ISBN 978-1-948691-41-3

Camping Around, U.S.A.

One

"In conclusion, it is the view of Union Station embassy that it would be too disruptive for EarthCent's local diplomatic presence for me to accept the honor of a six-month stay on our homeworld to substitute for President Beyer while he takes a well-deserved sabbatical."

"You won't consider changing your mind?" Libby asked when Kelly finished dictating her weekly report.

"If I made a list of the million things in the galaxy I hope never to do, standing in as the president of EarthCent while Stephen goes on sabbatical would be at the very top. And then what happens if he does a runner like his predecessor?"

"Is that your main objection? That President Beyer might flee and leave you holding the office?"

"I wouldn't say it was the first thing I thought of when the request came through. Maybe the second."

"While I was recording your voluminous list of reasons for refusing to serve as EarthCent's acting president, I couldn't help thinking they sounded more like excuses than professional objections," the Stryx librarian continued. "Perhaps you could distill them all into a single explanation that would make more sense for everybody involved."

The EarthCent ambassador sat silently for a minute, staring at her display desk, and then she looked up at the ceiling and said, "Because I don't want to."

"I gathered that much, but why don't you want to? If it's the fear that you'll be trapped in the president's job, I'm sure we could arrange safeguards."

"I'm sixty-seven years old, Libby, and I already have a hard time remembering where I left my notebook with all of the appointments and action items that I've written down so I don't forget them. It doesn't make sense for a diplomat with short-term-memory issues to change postings at this stage of life, and you know how the aliens prefer to deal with a familiar face."

"The Vergallians change ambassadors far more often than EarthCent."

"That's different," Kelly said. "The Vergallian ambassadors all have decades of royal training, so the other species understand who they're dealing with from day one. When I first came to Union Station, it took seven years before the aliens started inviting me to meetings where my attendance wasn't required by the tunnel network treaty."

"That had to do with their feelings about humanity in general, not about you in particular," Libby said. "Nobody can force you to accept the honor of acting as EarthCent's president, but I wouldn't want you to regret a hastily made decision after they find somebody else."

"What about my grandchildren? Six months at this time of their lives is like six years to them."

"I'm sure they'd be thrilled to see their grandmother at the head of EarthCent even though it's just temporary. And you could invite them to visit and see the birthplace of humanity while you're there."

"But the embassy will lose all continuity," Kelly protested. "Donna is retiring in two weeks, Ofer is going to start visiting other Stryx stations to interview our local staff for his history of EarthCent, and Daniel is chronically overworked with his Conference of Sovereign Human Communities."

"All issues that need to be addressed whether you are here or not," Libby said. "Perhaps you should view a six-month absence as an opportunity for your successors to prepare for the long run. It's a shame that your request for ambassadors over the age of sixty-five to be given the option of part-time employment is languishing in EarthCent's human resources department for want of the president's signature."

Kelly drew a sharp breath when the Stryx librarian's implication hit home. "Stephen has been sitting on my request to strong-arm me into taking his place while he goes on sabbatical?"

"I'm not sure that you can draw a direct line between the two, but as the acting president, it would certainly be within your power to approve the change."

"You're saying if I agree to go to Earth for six months I can transition to part-time when I get back to Union Station and continue as ambassador? What about Aabina?"

"Are you asking if her employment here will be affected by your replacing the president during his sabbatical?"

"I want to take her with me," Kelly said. "Working as the special assistant to the acting president of another species will look good on her résumé and I'm sure she'll enjoy the New World's Fair."

"I thought you were worried about how Daniel and Ofer would run the embassy without you," Libby reminded her. "Now you want them to do without Aabina as well?"

"Like you said, it will be a good experience for them to prepare for the long run. Daniel can get his wife to come in and help. She's only working part-time at SBJ Fashions these days."

"The sabbatical substitution rules do allow you to bring one member of your support staff, but you'll have to ask Aabina."

"No buts," Kelly said firmly. "It's Aabina or bust. Well, Aabina and Joe, but husbands can't count in quotas. And unlimited Stryxnet access while I'm on Earth. I'm too old to learn how to use whatever primitive information technology they have in the president's office. I need to be able to talk to you."

"You drive a hard bargain, Ambassador," the Stryx librarian said. "I'll agree to an open connection, but only from your temporary office. The holoconferencing system that the president uses to contact the embassies will remain a metered connection, even though we end up paying ourselves through the EarthCent subsidies. Are you ready to record a new conclusion to your weekly report?"

"Let me talk to Aabina first. And Joe. Maybe he won't want to go."

"I don't think that will be a problem. Aabina is in her office reviewing Ofer's travel schedule with him."

"Then I'll be right back." Kelly got up, waved open the security lock on her office door that she always engaged while making her weekly reports, and turned left in the lobby for her special assistant's office. Aabina's door was open, and from the volume of Ofer's voice, it sounded like they were having a serious disagreement.

"Ambassador," Aabina greeted Kelly, effectively putting the argument on pause. "How can I help you?"

"EarthCent wants me to fill in for the president on Earth while he takes a six-month sabbatical, and I made accepting conditional on your accompanying me."

"Yes."

"You'll go?"

"Yes."

"You don't need to think about it or check with your mother?" Kelly asked, knowing that the Vergallian girl's first loyalty had to be to the queen that Aabina was destined to one day replace.

"It's official EarthCent business, and six months is too short a time to require special clearance," Aabina said. "Besides, I wanted to visit the New World's Fair, and now I won't have to use any vacation time to get there."

"When are you leaving?" Ofer asked.

"Not for another two weeks," Kelly said. "You've been working for us almost a year now, and I'm confident that with Daniel's help, you won't have anything to worry about."

"I'm not worried. I want a promotion."

"But we just dropped 'acting' from your job title two months ago. For somebody with no work experience to go from unemployed to assistant consul in less than a year is unheard of."

"Ofer was just explaining to me that he wants to move into the diplomatic track," Aabina said. "He feels he needs the rank of consul if the other species are going to take him seriously."

"But you're too young," Kelly said immediately. "There's a minimum age to advance beyond—no?" she broke off when she noticed him shaking his head.

"I put in a request last week to have the minimum age for consul changed to twenty-five, and the president approved it," Ofer said. "After all, your son is only a year or two older than me and he's practically an emperor."

"So they changed the age requirement, but you know that all promotions of diplomatic staff come through channels, and I can't—what?" the ambassador interrupted herself.

"We received a tunneling network telegram from the president's office while you were doing your weekly report," Aabina told her. "Ofer's promotion is already in the works, but they want him to continue with the history."

"And I say that history belongs in the past," Ofer said in a heated voice. "If I learned one thing from studying nineteenth and twentieth-century political economy on Earth it's that nobody cares."

Kelly blinked several times as if she thought that her assistant consul had been replaced by an illusion. "But I hired you specifically to be EarthCent's historian."

"And my professional opinion is you don't need one. The Stryx librarians have records about everything of note EarthCent ambassadors have accomplished to date, and I've already condensed that into a not-very-interesting monograph. Going around to the other Stryx stations and interviewing ambassadors about the first time they accidentally poisoned themselves on something that looked like an apple at an alien embassy reception won't add anything to the academic value."

"He doesn't want to leave Jyndal, and Baa won't let her travel with him," Aabina explained.

"That's not it at all," Ofer said, his voice straining with emotion as he rose from his chair. "I mean, it's true I don't want to leave Jyndal alone. Both of us have had enough of that to last two lifetimes. But after being raised in solitude by an alien artificial intelligence I've become hyper-conscious about lost time. Why should I give another year of my life to something I don't believe in? If you don't think I'm good for anything other than writing about the past, I'll find another job."

"That's not what Aabina meant," Kelly told him, even as it struck her that this was the first time she'd ever seen her special assistant mishandle a situation. "It's just taken us both by surprise. You've been working diligently for the last year without complaining and we thought you were preparing to leave on your grand tour of EarthCent embassies. Now you're telling us that it's not worth the trouble."

"And that I want to be somebody who helps to shape the future, not some dusty academic."

"Does it have to be one or the other? I feel like you're giving us an ultimatum here, which is the last thing anybody wants to see in a diplomat."

"I'm just trying to be honest and not waste anybody's time," Ofer said. "Maybe I could write about EarthCent's transition to the Human Empire going forward, but I don't see the point of digging into the recent past."

"Your timing couldn't be any more awkward," Kelly said, half to herself. "Donna's retirement party is in two weeks, and then Aabina and I will be on Earth for six months. If you leave too, Daniel will be stuck running both the embassy and CoSHC with whatever last-minute replacements he can dig up."

"Tell the president that you changed your mind about the need for a historian, and that as consul, I'll be able to take some of the load off of Associate Ambassador Cohan while you're on Earth. If President Beyer needs you to replace him before he goes out on sabbatical, that means we have leverage."

"I'm sorry," Aabina said to Kelly. "Ofer asked me last week if any Earth texts about the exercise of power had been deemed worthy of translation into Vergallian and I told him about Machiavelli's *The Prince* and Sun Tzu's *Art of War*. It didn't occur to me that he was looking for a how-to manual."

"Are you sure this is what you want now, Ofer, or are you, Machiavelli, and Sun Tzu simply seizing the moment?" Kelly asked.

"Carpe diem," Aabina corrected the ambassador under her breath.

"Actually, it was your husband's idea," Ofer said, looking a little abashed for the first time. "I ask him for advice whenever you invite me over for dinner, and he said if I didn't want to dedicate my life to writing history, I should act now, rather than putting it off. It took me a month to work myself up to this."

"Why didn't you come to me rather than Joe if you were unhappy?" Kelly asked.

"You're the famous ambassador," Ofer said. "Half of the monograph about EarthCent's history that I wrote ended up being about events on Union Station. You don't know how intimidating you can be."

Kelly looked from Ofer to Aabina at a loss for words. Nearly a minute passed in silence while she mentally reviewed her interactions with the young man, and she realized that he had become increasingly deferential as she had answered questions for his history about the highlights of her thirty-plus years as the ambassador on Union Station.

"Let's start over and pretend I just came in," Kelly finally said. "Aabina, I've been asked to spend six months on Earth to replace the president while he goes on sabbatical and I'm hoping you'll come with me. Ofer, before I leave, we need to sit down and discuss your career path. It occurs to me that when we're together, I spend all my time talking about things I've done in the past, and I've never once asked you about your plans for the future."

"Can we talk about it now?" Ofer asked, confused by the ambassador's sudden shift in strategy, and unwilling to give up the initiative after having worked himself up to making demands. "Jyndal and I have been discussing our plans and we agreed that I can't continue on a path that will take me away from Union Station for long periods."

"Have you considered the diplomatic track?" Kelly tried again. "Although I hired you as a historian, you did pass the civil service exam, and EarthCent is suffering from a shortage of diplomatic personnel, particularly at the intermediate level. If we can get you promoted to consul, it would allow you to take some of the burden off Daniel while I'm on Earth."

"Uh, I guess I could try it for six months."

"Excellent. I'll include a request for your immediate promotion in my reply to the president. Aabina, could you join me in my office?"

The Vergallian rose from her desk and followed the ambassador back to her office. "Why did you capitulate?" Aabina asked as soon as the door slid closed behind them. "I like Ofer, but I'm not confident he has what it takes to engage with the other ambassadors without somebody holding his hand, and that could end up creating more work for Daniel."

"Did I ever tell you why I hired Ofer to be EarthCent's historian?" Kelly asked her special assistant.

"I thought you wanted somebody to get started and he fell into your lap."

"With a recommendation," the ambassador said, her eyes flicking toward the ceiling.

The Vergallian's lips formed a perfect O-shape. "All right," she said. "But it's still going to mean a rough six months for Daniel, especially since I'll be going with you. And with Donna and myself gone, who is going to deal with the *All Species Cookbook*? We can't keep up with the new releases from Earth because all our editorial and production assets are here on Union Station."

"Donna is recruiting a replacement for herself as we speak. Did she tell you who she's trying to persuade to take her job?"

"Judith," Aabina said. "She worked for EarthCent Intelligence until she had her third child. Do you think she'll be happy as embassy manager? Between helping Thomas run EarthCent Intelligence's training camp and the dueling hobby, I assessed her as more of the physical type."

"Donna tells me that acquiring a husband and children has given Judith an interest in cooking," Kelly said with a sly smile. "And don't forget that she's married to Bob Steelforth, the senior Union Station reporter for the Galactic Free Press. I wouldn't be surprised if she's more knowledgeable about what's happening around here than I am."

"All right," Aabina said, nodding in approval. "If she accepts the job, that will be a big help. But it took Donna and I working together to keep the cookbook updates running smoothly."

"And I'm sorry I just let you do it in addition to your work for me. It's time we hired a dedicated cookbook team, though I have in mind a couple of sisters who might be willing to take it on as a job share."

"Shaina and Brinda?"

"I don't see why not. Dorothy tells me that they've stepped back from SBJ Fashions."

Aabina hesitated uncharacteristically "Do you mind if I ask you a personal question?"

"Of course not," Kelly said.

"Why did you agree to replace the president for six months? I've heard you say a thousand times that you'd never accept a posting away from Union Station, and with the Human Empire moving towards its first milestone review, I would have thought you'd want to stay where you'd be best positioned to help."

"It recently came to my attention that President Beyer has been holding up my request to allow ambassadors over the age of sixty-five to cut their hours in half without losing seniority or benefits. Some days I feel like I don't have the energy to do this anymore, Aabina, but then I imagine waking up without any work to look forward to and I'm scared. If I grit my teeth and serve six months on Earth, I'll be able to shift to part-time when we get back and finish out my term."

"It's my fault," Aabina said. "As your special assistant, I should have shielded you from more—"

"I couldn't have lasted this long without you," Kelly interrupted. "And to be perfectly honest, the same party who wanted me to hire Ofer is pushing me to take the posting on Earth."

"Then I'm putting a condition on my accompanying you. No twelve-hour days, and if we're hosting a dinner or attending an event at one of the other embassies in the evening, you'll take the morning off."

"I intend to treat my time on Earth like the caretaker assignment that it is, though I'll try to get enough done to ensure that the president isn't buried in work when he returns."

"I'll hold you to that," Aabina said seriously. "And just because you're filling in for the president doesn't mean you can't take any time off. You have seven weeks of vacation in the bank, and it doesn't make sense to save them if you're reducing your hours to part-time when we return to Union Station."

"I didn't think of that, but you're right," Kelly said, her face brightening. "Maybe Joe will want to visit some of those historical Grenouthian theme parks we keep hearing about from people who have been to Earth recently."

"Are you ready to finish your weekly report?" Libby asked.

"What? Oh, I forgot," the EarthCent ambassador said. "In conclusion, it is the view of Union Station embassy that the president deserves his long-delayed sabbatical, and I would be honored to accept a six-month posting on Earth for myself, my husband, and my special assistant, Aabina, on the condition that President Beyer gives me his personal assurance that he won't take advantage and flee tunnel network space, like his predecessor."

"He's living on a Vergallian tech-ban world," Aabina commented.

"Who?"

"President Lin. He didn't leave the tunnel network."

"To tell you the truth, I'd almost forgotten him. Ofer asked me, and I said that President Lin had left the tunnel network because there wasn't any other mechanism to resign his office."

"I thought you knew," Aabina said. "Technically, he did leave tunnel network space by vacationing on a Fleet Vergallian world until the Stryx replaced him with President Beyer. Then he moved to a tech-ban planet in the Empire of a Hundred Worlds."

"It's funny, but I didn't know he was that close to your people. When we set up EarthCent Intelligence, one of President Lin's main concerns was that Vergallians were trying to take over Earth. Which reminds me. Did I give you our latest intelligence report about the Ladies in Waiting movement?"

"Yes, but it was just a summary of the reporting in the Galactic Free Press. There seems to be a growing schism in the movement between women who want to select queens from your own people and those who want to ask Vergallian princesses to come and serve as contract queens, like Affie is doing for the Alts here on Union Station."

"Well, we should have plenty of opportunity to figure out what's happening while we're on Earth," Kelly said. "I'll take notes."

Two

"Are you sure you only want Chicken Cacciatore?" Kevin asked the trader. "I know it's the best squeeze tube meal for Zero G, but the Eggplant Parmesan is a close second, and the Chili con Carne—"

"They aren't all for me," the trader interrupted with a laugh. "I use them as throw-ins to close deals with miners when I visit habitats. I've tried bringing a variety in the past, but as soon as you run out of a particular entrée, everybody starts asking for it. Plus, I'm assuming there's a discount for taking a gross."

"I don't have a hundred and forty-four squeeze tubes of Chicken Cacciatore in stock, but I can ping the distributor and have them here in two hours. Can you wait that long?"

"I'll take a nap. Half off?"

"My margins aren't that good," Kevin protested. "At half off the individual squeeze-tube price, I'd be losing money. I could do thirty percent."

"My next stop is Flower, and I heard a rumor that she's getting into the Zero-G rations business."

"Figures, but it doesn't change my cost unless I start buying from her. Hey, do you want to take a few packages to her for me?"

"Forty percent," the trader said, unable to hide a smile. "I'll throw in hand-delivery as long as all of the packages are going the same place and they aren't too heavy."

Kevin took a minute to calculate his profit on forwarding the packages against the hard bargain on the squeeze tubes, which were basically break-even at forty percent off.

"Three delivery locations on Flower, but they're just large envelopes, hardly any weight at all," he countered.

"And an apple."

"Deal."

As the trader headed back to her ship munching on the apple, Kevin pinged in the order for a gross of Chicken Cacciatore squeeze tubes. He took advantage of the opportunity to restock all his other Zero G rations, earning a bigger quantity discount than he had used to compute his profit. Then he saw his wife emerging from the converted storage container they called home and walking directly towards the chandlery with their two-year-old son in her arms.

"Daddy," Richard cried, extending both arms over the counter for his father to take him.

"Good morning, Ricky," Kevin said. "Got any big plans for the day?"

"Helping Daddy," Dorothy answered for their son. "I forgot that it's a Take-Your-Daughter-to-Work Day, so Margie is coming with me as soon as she can decide what to wear. It wouldn't be fair to her to bring them both, even though Richard spends most of his time in the office nursery."

"That's fine," Kevin said. "Your dad is getting ready to leave for six months on Earth and he wants to talk me through all of his pending deals so I can make good if Paul isn't around. I'm going to write them down."

"Good luck with that. Dad has been making verbal contracts with every small ship owner to camp in Mac's Bones for the last forty years. He probably has hundreds of deals on a back burner."

"Fortunately, the small ship owners who are honorable enough to pay their debts don't need contracts to remind them. And if Joe could convert all of the goodwill he's stored up with small ship owners into creds, your mother could retire now and skip the whole trip to Earth."

"You know my mom doesn't need the pension from EarthCent anymore. She just likes complaining about the full retirement age for diplomats being seventy-five when the support staffers make their full pension after forty years. Donna started as a teenager, and she could have retired years ago."

"Donna could have retired soon after her daughters founded InstaSitter," Kevin said. "I bet her pension payments will go directly to charity."

"You have it backward," Dorothy said. "Donna and Stanley have always lived on their income, just like my parents. Would you accept money from Margie and Richard when we're retired?"

"No, I suppose not. Besides, the way SBJ Fashions is growing, you're going to be my sugar momma. Have you looked at how the royalty payments for some of your designs are piling up in the Thark accounts we set up for the kids?"

"That's their money, not ours. But I did look the other day, and it seems like the balance is rising faster than the payments."

"That's thanks to your mother's connections. When I went to set up the accounts at their off-world betting parlor, the Thark ambassador was there, and he offered to mirror the portfolio he runs for the less adventurous members of his family. The money is being used for insurance underwriting."

"Isn't insurance risky?" Dorothy asked.

"Not for the Tharks," Kevin said. "They've been making book on everything for millions of years. If the Thark ambassador was here right now, he could give you odds on what Margie will be wearing when she finally comes out that door."

"She knows I work in the fashion industry, and she wants to make an impression."

"But she stops in the office to see you every day after school."

"This is an official Take-Your-Daughter-to-Work Day, so it's dress-up," Dorothy said. "All of the girls in Libby's school will give an oral report to their class."

"Doesn't seem fair to the boys," Kevin said.

"I think that's part of the lesson." She pointed at her ear a moment to indicate she was communicating via her implant. "Oops, that was Libby. I have to go."

"She didn't approve of your characterization of her teaching?"

"No. Margie needs me to help her pick out a hat that goes with the dress."

Dietro was waiting in the reception area when Dorothy and her daughter arrived at the offices of SBJ Fashions. "Did you forget about our meeting?" he demanded before noticing the girl and softening his voice. "You look lovely today, Margret Anne Crick."

"Thank you," Margie said, dropping her best curtsy.

"What meeting?" Dorothy asked, confirming the Vergallian's suspicions. "Oh, wait. Is this about the New World's Fair?"

"The biggest event on Earth since the Stryx opening and it slipped your mind?" Dietro asked.

"If you're forgetting things, Mommy, you should write them down like grandma," Margie said seriously. "Are we going to have a meeting, Mister Dietro?"

"Now that your mother is here, yes." He glanced at Dorothy, and then crouched to bring his eyes to the same level as the seven-year-old's. "It's an important meeting and the conferencing time is expensive, so please don't ask questions until it's over. Okay?"

"Doesn't Uncle Jeeves pay for everything?"

"Brilliant observation," Jeeves said, floating out of the conference room where he'd been waiting for Dorothy's arrival. "You only have five minutes to get accustomed to the headsets before our window of time opens. Fortunately, I had the foresight to order extras in children's sizes."

"What headsets?" Dorothy asked. "Aren't we going to do a holoconference?"

"Virtual reality visors and avatars cut the bandwidth requirements by over ninety percent, so it brings the cost on par with a voice-only Stryxnet conference. The headsets were developed for gaming on Earth and have been modified for VR conferencing by programmers from Bits working on Flower. Let's get you acclimated to the virtual environment now so you're ready when the call starts."

Jeeves led the way into the conference room and hovered behind Margie as she removed her hat and donned the virtual reality headset.

"Are you sure this isn't too heavy for her?" Dorothy asked as she adjusted her own visor with the extensions that wrapped around the ears.

"The children's sizes look like the originals manufactured on Earth a century ago, but they're fabricated on

Flower using modern Dollnick technology," Jeeves reassured her. "They weigh less than that fashionable hat with the artificial fruit that Margie was wearing when she came in."

"I already enabled the headphones for ambient sound, so we'll be able to hear each other talking outside of the holoconference as well as in," Dietro said. "We don't have much time, so strap the hand controllers on your wrists and pick one of the short demonstrations from the beginner's menu you'll see to the right. Margie, I don't know if you've ever used eye movements to navigate—"

"I've patched in to navigate for her," Jeeves said. "You choose, Margie. Do you want to ride the choo-choo or the merry-go-round?"

"The ponies."

"Why didn't I get a choo-choo?" Dorothy complained. "I don't want to do a roller coaster or downhill skiing. I'll get motion sick."

"Just pick something or you'll get motion sick in the meeting the first time your avatar turns its head," Dietro told her. "If you want to skip the canned demos, select 'Local' mode and you can interact with my avatar."

"Done," Dorothy said, choosing the option with practiced eye movements. She found herself in a virtual reality version of the SBJ Fashions conference room, complete with a table, chairs, and coffee station. Sitting across from her was an avatar of a handsome Vergallian that looked so much like Dietro she could have picked it out of a crowd, and an accurate version of Jeeves floated next to an avatar of Margie that could have been drawn by a professional cartoonist.

"You can thank me later for commissioning Daniel and Shaina's son to produce your avatars," Jeeves said. "I find that it's impossible to take the default versions seriously."

"What do I look like?" Dorothy asked, trying to look down at herself, but all she could see was the front of her dress which abruptly cut off around her waist. "Where are my legs?"

"You aren't wearing ankle controllers, so the avatar is only half-enabled," Dietro explained. He stood up from his chair and began walking around the table, though to Dorothy, it looked like his upper torso was floating on air. "We're going to be sitting in this meeting, but if it had been a walking-around thing—" he bent over and did something that almost gave the impression he was preparing for a headstand, and then all of a sudden his legs appeared in fashionable pants that matched his suit jacket, "—I would have given you and Margie ankle controllers as well."

"How come all of Jeeves is showing?"

"What makes you think that all of me is ever showing?" the young Stryx asked.

"All right," Dietro said. "We're meeting with Helen, who's been operating pop-up boutiques for nanofabric fittings on Earth for the last year under the brand Tunnel Network Tailors. We lucked out on the timing and she's available to manage our booth at the Human Empire pavilion."

"Will my brother or somebody else from Human Empire headquarters be on the call?" Dorothy asked. "Who's in charge there?"

"Larry, their Minister of Trade, is responsible for the New World's Fair pavilion, and he's on Earth. When I talked with him last week, he introduced me to his assistants, Scott and Dwight, and my guess is that one of them will be on the call. The fair is opening next week so I imagine they're running around putting out fires."

"What's the big clock?" Margie asked, bobbing her head and shoulders in time with music only she could hear as she rode a carousel pony that only she could see.

"Our meeting is about to begin," Jeeves told her. "Do you want to listen while the adults talk about marketing fashions on Earth, or would you rather stay on the merry-go-round?"

"Ponies."

"Thirty seconds," Dietro said. "Helen is the one who requested this meeting, so don't be surprised if it's a pitch."

"A sales pitch? To us?" Dorothy asked.

The Vergallian's avatar shrugged. "If it was just a question of a little cash for the booth, she would have told me rather than asking to see the top management."

"But Shaina and Brinda aren't here."

"You and Dietro have our full confidence, and Baa said she couldn't be bothered," Jeeves told them.

"Then why are you here?" Dorothy asked.

"Technical support."

Two new avatars arrived at the table, an athletic middle-aged woman, and a short man in his late twenties. "Helen, Dwight," Dietro greeted them. "You're live with Dorothy—" he pointed across the table by way of an introduction, "and Jeeves. We may be joined at some point by Margie, who is here for Take-Your-Daughter-to-Work Day, but she's currently occupied in another part of virtual reality."

Both the newcomers glanced nervously at Jeeves and decided to keep their eyes on Dorothy instead.

"You won't remember me, but we met at a franchisee sign-up event I attended on Union Station," Helen said to the EarthCent ambassador's daughter. "I was returning from a fabric buying trip to a Frunge open world when I had a layover on the station and attended the event at the Empire Convention Center. Your demonstration changed my life."

"I'm so happy to hear that," Dorothy said. "Changing lives and making the galaxy a better place is why we're in this business. We're excited that you'll be demonstrating our nanofabric fittings at the New World's Fair, and I'll be surprised if you aren't the hit of the Human Empire pavilion."

"You'll have some tough competition from Flower, including a booth demonstrating this virtual reality conferencing technology," Dwight said with a grin. "But we do believe that the Human Empire pavilion will be one of the fair's main attractions."

"Which is what I wanted to talk to you about," Helen said. "I have a universal nanofabric garment from my own franchise, plus the one Dietro sent for the booth, but I've been watching documentaries about fairs, and I'm worried it's not enough."

"The nanofabric is practically indestructible," Dietro assured her. "You won't wear it out."

"That's not the problem. I've already trained half a dozen assistants to help with fittings, but it occurred to me that your experience demonstrating the technology at trade fairs has been to sign up franchisees, not to sell dresses. When women came into my boutique, I never spent less than fifteen minutes on a fitting, and some of them would have stayed all day trying different looks if I hadn't set up an appointment schedule to keep them moving."

"But you'll be able to do two fittings at the same time, which is more than we ever—" Dorothy cut herself off when she noticed Helen's avatar shaking its head. "What am I thinking? Of course, you're right. We don't just want crowds of people standing around watching you demonstrate the nanofabric. We want to sell dresses."

"Helen asked us if it's possible to expand her booth space at this late date, and luckily for you, we had a last-minute cancellation by a musical instrument manufacturer from an open world," Dwight said. "You can triple the size of your booth, but I have to get a decision this morning because we're running out of time."

"Are you confident you can staff and manage it?" Dietro asked, his avatar facing Helen's.

"Yes," the boutique manager said. "I may have to pay some overtime the first couple of days, but I have a list longer than my arm of women who want to get into the business. Can I tell them that working in the SBJ Fashion's booth for the fair will give them a leg up at being approved as franchisees when it's over?"

"We'll be happy to have them, but there's the whole territory thing," Dorothy said. "We wouldn't want them all opening boutiques on the same street."

"And we discussed you taking the information of anybody interested in opening a franchise," Dietro's avatar said to Helen's. "I've been thinking that rather than waiting until the end of the New World's Fair to make contact and invite them to Union Station, we should schedule regular training and recruitment events on Earth. Is that something you think you could handle once activity at the fair settles into a regular pattern?"

"You're asking me to train new franchisees for you rather than just pass along their information?" Helen asked.

Her avatar frowned. "We didn't talk about that when we agreed on my compensation package."

"This would be extra," Dietro said. "And you'd need some assistants—how many do you usually bring to a demonstration, Dorothy?"

"At least two," Dorothy said. "One to act as a model before we start taking volunteers from the audience, and another one at the back of the room to sign people in."

"Even with your triple space, the booths aren't that big, and we can't allow you to start setting up chairs in the aisles," Dwight interjected. "If you're planning on demonstrations for an invited audience, rather than fair attendees who happen to be circulating through the pavilion, we'll have to ask you to rent a space elsewhere."

"Let's wait and see how many people express an interest," Dietro said. "If it's not too many, inviting them to Union Station with partly subsidized travel expenses may be a way to winnow out the curiosity seekers. But if you're getting people signing up every day, we'll pay for you to rent a conference room at a hotel whenever the numbers add up to a good crowd."

"It's not something I've been trained for," Helen objected. "I attended the one demonstration, and you sold me on applying for a franchise, but I've never done that sort of recruiting myself."

"Dorothy will come for the first one and show you," Jeeves said.

"On Earth?" Dorothy's avatar demanded, rising to its nonexistent feet.

"Somebody forgot their ankle controllers," Dwight said.

"You know Flazint won't go, and Affie can't leave the station for that long while she's contract-queening," Dietro said. "Myst and Lancelot might be willing, and they have experience as your assistants, but both are studying at the Open University and the semester just started. I suppose Shaina and Brinda might do it for a lark if they want to visit Earth."

A little girl in a white summer dress suddenly popped into the holoconference, and Margie said, "Grandma is going to Earth. We can visit."

"There you go," Jeeves said. "A perfect excuse to take the family on vacation at my expense."

Dorothy scowled at the Stryx, and her expression was accurately reproduced in virtual reality. "You coached her, didn't you?"

"The merry-go-round didn't go anywhere," Margie said. "And the same song played again and again."

"Maybe there won't be many sign-ups," Helen said. "I doubt people will be attending the fair because they're looking for a career change."

"I wouldn't bet on that," Dwight said. "It changed my career three months before the opening date. I was working for an event planning consultant in the city that the Human Empire hired last year to set up their pavilion. Then Larry, the Minister of Trade, showed up, fired my boss, and hired me and my friend to work for him."

"I don't know," Dorothy said. "Kevin would have to close the chandlery while we're gone, and he'll be covering a lot of things for my dad."

"Nothing that won't wait a week or two, and I'll help Paul if things get too busy," Jeeves said.

"It's like you want me off the station for some reason."

"Why is the clock back?" Margie asked.

"Thirty seconds," Dwight said. "We'll be putting that extra booth space on SBJ's account, and you know where to find me if there are any questions."

"And I really could use the extra nanofabric yesterday since I'm going to have to train more salespeople," Helen said.

"Do we have it in stock?" Dorothy asked Dietro.

"Gem production is running smoothly now," the sales manager replied. "I'll just allocate another half dozen for Earth and increase the next order."

"My mom has to be there for the fair opening, so I'll get my dad to bring it to you," Dorothy's avatar told Helen. "He likes being useful."

Three

"Where's Kelly?" Daniel asked Donna. "Something must have happened for her to be late to your retirement party."

The embassy manager did a little tilt with her head to indicate that the ambassador was in her office. "She got a bit emotional and needed some privacy. We've been working together for almost thirty-five years and it's difficult for her to let go."

"Mom's younger than Kelly and she gets to retire first," Chastity said with a laugh as she handed the associate ambassador a glass of champagne. "And what's your excuse for being late?"

"Union Station Gambling Commission," Daniel told the owner of the Galactic Free Press. "I should have known I was in trouble when the other ambassadors voted me a permanent seat on the Contract Labor Committee."

"What does gambling have to do with contracts?"

"Nothing, so far. But it turns out that the sole qualification for sitting on a tunnel network commission is holding a permanent seat on an ambassadorial-level committee. I didn't have the sense to pretend I was out when the Thark Ambassador stopped in this morning and asked if I could spare a little time. Speaking of which, I missed lunch."

"There's plenty to eat in the conference room, and you could delegate Ofer to attend some of Kelly's meetings in her place," Donna said. "It requires a quorum for a committee to take action, so it's not like he can do any harm. Kelly has been bringing Ofer to her meetings for the last year and the ambassadors all know him."

The Drazen ambassador took Daniel's place, produced a bouquet of chrysanthemums and lilies from behind his back, and presented it to Donna with his tentacle. "Congratulations on successfully completing your job," Bork said. "Do you have plans for a second career?"

"Other than grandmothering?" Donna asked. "I'll be available for consulting to get Judith up to speed in the embassy, but I can't work more than ten hours a week or EarthCent will start reducing my pension by half of the additional amount I earn. And I'll continue running our dance mixer and a few other volunteer programs I set up for the human community over the years."

"I shall look forward to seeing you on those occasions you happen to be here, not that I expect to visit as often in Kelly's absence."

"Leave it to a Drazen to bring a funeral arrangement to a retirement party," a voice interrupted in scratchy English. The Frunge ambassador pushed past Bork and extended a small box to Donna. "I did a little research and I believe you'll find my gift more appropriate to the situation."

"Jewelry?" Donna asked, her eyes lighting up. She tucked the bouquet into the crook of her arm and accepted the box. "It's too heavy for a ring, but the box is wrong for a necklace."

"Open it," Czeros said. "I saved the receipt just in case."

"A pocket watch? It's very handsome. If the case is solid gold, you really shouldn't have."

"I was afraid the value would go over EarthCent's allowable amount, so I went with brass."

"I thought brass was much lighter than gold," Donna said, weighing the watch in her hand. "The mechanism behind the glass is lovely."

"Fake," Czeros told her. "The brass is alloyed with just enough depleted uranium to mass the same as gold, though it's easy enough to spot with a sensitive Geiger counter. And what looks like a mechanism is actually a Dollnick display showing simulated clockwork, just like Kelly's decorative wristwatch. Don't worry, the radioactivity is well within the safety limits for your species so long as you don't carry multiple pocket watches at the same time."

"Thank you," the embassy manager said, hastily placing both gifts on her soon-to-be-former desk. "Did you enter through the conference room? The refreshments are self-serve."

"We'll be right back," Bork said over his shoulder as he took off across the lobby behind Czeros.

"Did you ever imagine that alien ambassadors would attend your retirement party?" Blythe asked her mother. "You've come a long way from a pregnant teenage newlywed on her first trip away from Earth."

"Did I ever tell you that the consul I worked for before Kelly arrived was an alcoholic?" Donna asked her daughters. "Libby used to let me know when he passed out in bars so I could send your father to take him home."

"You always told us that he was sick," Chastity said.

"It was a sickness with him. I'll never understand how the Stryx went about picking diplomats for the first half-century of EarthCent's existence."

"Or how they chose a teenager to keep the consulate running."

"The two of you launched InstaSitter when you were younger than I was when I started working here," Donna pointed out. "Who could have imagined then where you'd be today?"

"Oh, I suspect a certain Stryx librarian had a pretty good idea," Blythe said, and lifted her champagne glass toward the ceiling in a mock toast.

A stunning Vergallian slipped past Donna's daughters and presented the retiring embassy manager with a flat rectangular package. "You don't have to open it now," Ambassador Aleeytis said. "I know you've been running EarthCent's social mixer for decades so I thought you might like an official ballroom dance card. It supports up to a thousand couples, including scoring and random pairings for speed dating."

"That's so thoughtful of you," Donna said. "Thank you."

"In the interest of full disclosure, an amount to purchase a retirement gift for you was left behind by my predecessor with a note of the date of your departure on the embassy calendar. Aabina's mother appreciates everything you've done to make it comfortable for her daughter to work in your embassy."

"Still, thank you for the thought."

"I brought you chocolate," the Gem ambassador said, pressing in from the other side and placing a large box on Donna's desk. "Don't open it unless I'm here."

"I think I need to sit down." Donna fanned her face with one hand while pulling her chair out from under the reception desk with the other. "I didn't think I would get emotional, but you've all been so kind."

After failing to work his way through the crowd in the embassy lobby, Daniel exited to the corridor and walked next door to CoSHC headquarters so he could enter the shared conference room from the other side. The space around the buffet was packed with diplomats and other guests, but fortunately, the Verlock ambassador noticed when Daniel came in and made a space at the table for the associate ambassador to approach.

"Thank you," Daniel said, seizing the opportunity to grab the last burrito from a tray that a miraculously agile caterer was removing. He carefully took a bite while looking for a clean plate or a napkin to keep from losing beans and rice onto the floor.

"Just the person I wanted to see," Srythlan said slowly as he handed Daniel a plate. "Did Ambassador McAllister tell you about her commitment to the Galactic Historical Sites Commission?"

Rather than speak with his mouth full and risk spitting rice on the Verlock ambassador, Daniel shook his head.

"It must have slipped her mind with all the last-minute preparations to temporarily replace your president on Earth. The Historical Commission rotates through the Stryx stations and now it's our turn in the crater."

"Crater?" Daniel asked after hastily swallowing.

"Verlocks have a saying that history is the volcano that produces the land we stand on," Srythlan said. "Attempting to preserve history is akin to descending into a crater."

"I'm not sure I understand the analogy, but perhaps Ofer will." He took another bite of the burrito and waited to see if the Verlock ambassador would pick up on the hint.

"I understand that it will be difficult for you to meet all of your obligations while filling Kelly's shoes, but I'm afraid that the Historical Commission is a favorite of the Stryx, and they leave no wiggle room. The senior diplomat from each tunnel network species on the station is required to sit on the commission, though you could have Ofer substitute when you aren't available as long as it's not too frequent."

"How often will we meet?" Daniel asked, having had ample time to chew and swallow several bites during the ambassador's slow explanation.

"The schedule will depend on the agenda which will be discussed after the first meeting," Srythlan told him. "There's usually a site inspection involved, sometimes more than one."

"Do you mean interstellar travel? I can't just take off for weeks at a time!"

"These things take a number of meetings to plan so it's possible that Ambassador McAllister will have returned by then. As the Commission's chair, I've asked the Stryx librarian to send everyone scheduling details. Now if you'll excuse me, I still haven't offered my congratulations to Donna on her termination."

"Retirement," Daniel called after the Verlock, and found that his appetite had suddenly diminished more than could be explained by the lukewarm ingredients of the burrito. He ignored the notification from his implant that an informational packet had arrived and finished his late lunch while trying to figure out where he was going to find the time to sit on two new commissions with all the preparatory reading that entailed.

"You look like somebody who needs a clone," the Gem ambassador said to him as she helped herself to some cookies. "Did Srythlan just tell you about the Historical Commission?"

"A few hours now and then I could manage, but he said there could be site visits," Daniel said plaintively. "That could mean weeks away from Union Station."

"Some ambassadors consider an all-expenses-paid vacation on a Stryx science ship to be quite a perk."

"They send a science ship? My sister-in-law traveled to Cayl space on a science ship belonging to Stryx Vrine a couple of decades ago, and after the Alts demonstrated interstellar travel, the tunnel network delegation to their homeworld traveled on a science ship run by Stryx Wylx. But those were special occasions, and I'm surprised that an archeological expedition qualifies."

"I'm embarrassed to admit that Maker Dring asked the Stryx to send a science ship to the Gem homeworld to pick me up so I could attend that ball he organized for Kelly," Gwendolyn told the associate ambassador. "I just wanted to say that if you need help with the *All Species Cookbook* while Kelly is away, I've been coming to all of the open tastings, and I'm quite familiar with the procedures. Like many a Gem who grew up on a factory nutrition drink, I've become an avid amateur cook, and Human ingredients are the lowest common denominator."

"Thank you," Daniel said. "My wife, Shaina, and her sister, Brinda, will be taking care of the cookbook while Kelly and Aabina are away, so that's one thing I don't have to worry about. I'm sure they're around here if you want me to introduce you."

"I know both of them from SBJ Fashions," the Gem Ambassador said. "My little sister, Myst, works there part-time."

"Then I'll—what is it?" Daniel asked Ofer when the young consul appeared at his elbow with a distraught expression.

"Excuse me, Ambassadors," Ofer said. "There's a delegation of entertainment people here from Timble who say that they have a meeting scheduled in your office, Daniel."

"Where are they?"

"I took them back around through the corridor to the Conference of Sovereign Human Communities shared space and engaged the security lock," he pointed at the door that allowed the embassy and CoSHC to share the conference room, "so they wouldn't wander into the party."

"Elias again." Daniel groaned in exasperation and turned back to the Gem ambassador. "I'm sorry, but my office manager quit last week to get married and move to an open world with a saleswoman who stopped in to use our shared space. That makes the fourth office manager I've lost in a year. After three women, I thought I'd try a man, but he didn't even last two months. I guess in all the excitement he forgot to add a few appointments to the calendar."

"I can't imagine trying to run an office with the turnover Humans take for granted," Gwendolyn said sympathetically. "I'll see you tonight at the Historical Commission if you don't make it back to the party."

"Tonight?"

"Didn't you receive the informational package? Libby sent them out five minutes ago and the first meeting is scheduled for twenty-three hundred hours on your Human Standard Time."

"Then it sounds like after I put out the latest fire I'm going home for a nap," Daniel said, and started working his way through the crowd to the corridor exit.

Ofer remained behind with the Gem ambassador staring at her openly.

"I can't get over how much Myst looks like you," he finally said. "Whenever I go to see Jyndal at work and Myst is there, I wonder if I've entered a time warp."

"The Stryx assure us that there's no such thing as a time warp, and as clones, Myst and I should look alike, even though she's much younger than I am."

"Kelly told me I should sit next to you at meetings if there's an open seat," Ofer continued in his usual blunt manner. "I've been promoted to consul, but I don't really understand a lot of what goes on, so I hope you don't mind questions."

"You're welcome to ask all of the questions you want, and if you can subvocalize, Libby can silently relay them to me during meetings," Gwendolyn told him. "But I'm sure the reason Kelly asked you to sit next to me is that most of the ambassadors prefer not getting too close to clones. Haven't you noticed that we're standing in a bubble?"

Ofer looked around and his eyes widened in surprise. "I hadn't, but that's great. I'm still getting used to being around people, and parties are hard for me with the crowds. Do you mind if I stay close to you?"

"Not at all," the Gem said with a laugh. "I've never thought of making other sentients uncomfortable as a superpower, but it does have its uses. And as long as you're here, maybe you can clear up a translation issue for me. I thought that consuls were appointed to consulates."

"That's what I thought when they hired me, but Donna explained that with EarthCent, it's strictly a ranking thing. Embassies are usually run by an ambassador or an acting ambassador, but they invented the rank of associate ambassador for Daniel when they wanted to promote him from an assistant but were worried that two ambassadors at the same embassy would be too confusing. And junior diplomats all start as assistant consuls or junior assistant consuls."

"It seems a bit haphazard."

"It is, but nobody can be bothered to fix it," Ofer said. "I've only been with EarthCent for a year, but it's obvious even to me that everybody, right up to the ambassador level, is waiting for the Human Empire to take over. For the older ambassadors, like Kelly, it doesn't matter because they'll retire. But there's a discussion board where all of the younger diplomats chat, and whenever I bring up an institutional problem, everybody else tells me it's not worth fixing when the whole bureaucracy is going to be replaced in a few years."

"And you bring up problems on a regular basis?"

"At least once a week."

"I was under the impression that when the Human Empire meets its milestones it's going to take over EarthCent's diplomatic service intact," the Gem ambassador said. "It seems to me that pushing problems down the road can't be an effective strategy."

"That's what I keep telling them." Ofer lowered his voice a little, and added, "Sometimes I think that EarthCent has trouble attracting young talent. The other junior diplomats I talk to seem to get all of their information from Vergallian dramas and Grenouthian documentaries."

Gwendolyn laughed again. "Too much drama is a hazard for young Gem as well," she told him. "Myst has been awake for two years now, and she still dreams about designing jewelry for princesses. Though, to be perfectly fair, she got the obsession from reading Human fairytales in Dorothy's picture books when they were little."

"Myst doesn't sleep? I know that you're aliens but I figured you just followed a different clock."

"I should have said that Myst came out of stasis two years ago," the Gem ambassador said. "She was the same age as Dorothy when they were children, but when we recovered enough genetic material from the Farlings to start cloning males of our species, Myst chose to go into stasis until they matured. Lancelot is a first-generation male, and they're engaged to be married when they finish university."

"I wish I was engaged to be married," Ofer said wistfully. "After all, Jyndal and I are older than Myst and Lancelot, and I won't live nearly as long as they will."

"Have you asked her?"

"Every time we met until she told me to stop. Jyndal would take me in a second if it was up to her, but she signed an apprenticeship contract with Baa that prohibits marriage until she manages a major enchantment."

Gwendolyn couldn't help making a face. "Do you have a timeline?"

"Baa says that Jyndal needs to have a breakthrough first and it's almost impossible to predict," Ofer said sadly. "The next time Flower stops at Union Station, I'm going to ask M793qK to freeze my sperm."

"I'm going to pretend I didn't hear that," said a woman in her late thirties who had just arrived at the buffet.

"Judith," Gwendolyn greeted her. "I heard you're going to be replacing Donna."

"Ambassador Gem?" Judith asked uncertainly. "I'm going on context here because, you know…"

"We all look alike. Congratulations on the new job. I was just telling Associate Ambassador Cohan that I always come for the *All Species Cookbook* recipe testing days and I'm available to help."

"Why are you going to pretend you didn't hear me telling Ambassador Gem that I want to have my sperm frozen?" Ofer asked Judith. "It's not like I was spilling a diplomatic secret."

"I'm eating," the new embassy manager replied. "You must be the young consul Donna warned me about."

"Why did she warn you? I thought Donna liked me," Ofer said, standing on his toes to try to see the retiring embassy manager over the crowd.

"It's a figure of speech, not literal, and that's what she warned me about," Judith said while reloading her plate from a newly arrived bowl of salad. "I was told that you were raised by artificial intelligence and that you haven't quite mastered what topics of conversation are appropriate in which settings. Most people wouldn't talk about spilling secrets, or seed, while eating at a buffet."

"But I'm not eating."

"And that you take everything literally."

"It's a nice change," the Gem ambassador said. "One of the hardest parts about communicating with sentients from other species is adjusting to all of the cultural norms."

"All right," Judith said, turning to face the two of them. "We're going to be working together, and if you think it's important that I know about your most intimate secrets, I suppose the least I can do is listen."

"But it's not a secret," Ofer said. "I'm worried that I'll be too old before Baa lets my girlfriend marry me."

"How old is she now?"

"Twenty-two."

Judith paused with a forkful of salad halfway to her mouth and then shook her head. "We aren't going to solve this at a party, and it doesn't sound like an emergency situation, but Monday morning I want to see you and your girlfriend in my—in your office, and we'll get to the bottom of this."

"I think I like her," Ofer said to the Gem ambassador as the new embassy manager began elbowing her way through the crowd to find a clear space to eat her salad in peace.

Four

"Welcome, welcome," President Beyer said, coming forward to meet Kelly and Joe as soon as they entered the office. "Welcome to EarthCent Headquarters. Did you find it without any problem?"

"The floater autopilot took us right to the front of the building and dropped us off," Joe said.

"I can't get over how noisy the city is," Kelly added. "Haven't they ever heard of Dollnick acoustic suppression fields?"

"You'll get used to it and then you'll wonder why Union Station is so quiet when you get home," the president said. "Where is your charming Vergallian assistant?"

"Aabina wasn't willing to trust the floater to bring our luggage to the guest quarters. She said that there was a story in the Galactic Free Press warning visitors coming to Earth for the New World's Fair about trusting automated delivery systems."

"The floater operators that have been certified by the Elevator Transit Authority are probably trustworthy, but I'd be careful about some of the apps for floater sharing. Now come, let me show you my—your office."

"Don't you have any support staff?" the EarthCent ambassador asked, looking around the underwhelming office with a creeping feeling of dread.

"Hildy is always here, but she went to the guest house to wait in case you stopped there first, and of course, she's going on sabbatical with me. And both of our personal assistants have exercised their option to take their sabbaticals at the same time. Other than our new receptionist, who should be back from lunch any minute, you'll have the whole office to yourself."

"I don't understand, Stephen," Kelly said. "How can you operate EarthCent with so little staff?"

"We scattered our offices around the world so the legacy nations and city-states wouldn't think we were playing favorites," the president explained. "The training school you went to back in the day has been moved to Europe, our human resources operates out of India, and we have an office in every political entity with over twenty million citizens."

"That's the same number the Stryx use as a cutoff for connecting a tunnel to a world. Is there a relation?"

The president ushered Kelly and Joe into a corner office with a view of similar offices in several nearby skyscrapers and stood against the bookshelf while gesturing for Kelly to take the seat at his desk. "We began with ten million, but around a decade ago when retirees started moving back to Earth and young people stopped leaving in droves, we upped the number."

"Should I wait outside while you do your secret EarthCent stuff?" Joe asked. "I still have an intelligence clearance, but it doesn't get me very far in the embassy."

"Kelly is already in the system so there's nothing to do," the president said. "A technician from the Verlock embassy stopped in a few days ago and installed an unlimited bandwidth connection to the Stryxnet, but I couldn't think of a way to test it."

"Libby?" Kelly asked.

"Welcome to Earth, Ambassador," the Stryx station librarian responded. "I agreed to the open connection because you made it a condition of substituting for President Beyer, but it's an unprecedented situation, and I ask you to be judicious about contacting me."

"Message received. I don't want to get you in trouble with your elders."

"I thought you wanted the open Stryxnet connection so you could chat with your grandchildren," the president said with a laugh.

"My memory isn't what it once was, and even if I could learn to work with your information technology in six months, it would just be one more thing to forget when I go home," Kelly said defensively.

"I've lost track of how many times EarthCent has upgraded our systems with hand-me-downs from the aliens in just the last few years." Stephen reached into his pants pocket and pulled out what appeared to be a small tab. "I stopped trying to keep up and I just use my smartphone for everything."

"I can't believe anybody still manufactures those things," Joe said. "I had one when I was a teenager, but I grew up on a farm, and coverage in our area was so bad that it only worked around the house where we had a satellite connection."

"It's almost impossible to live in the city without one. The only place that you can catch a rental floater without using an app to summon it is at the Elevator Transit Authority spaceport where they expect tourists from the tunnel network."

"Are they expensive?" Kelly asked.

"Check the top left-hand drawer."

The EarthCent ambassador opened the drawer that the president indicated and found a dozen phones from every color of the rainbow slotted into a gang charger. "I get to pick one?"

"Pick three, they're all the same model, and you'll want Joe and Aabina to each have one," Stephen said. "They aren't secure by any stretch of the imagination, but we have a service that remotely accesses them once a week to check for spyware."

"I'll take the black one," Joe said. "Will the battery outlast our stay on Earth, or will we have to bring them back to charge at some point?"

"It depends on your usage but figure every three days at the minimum. There will be a charger just like this in your guest house as well as any hotel rooms if you travel."

"We should buy a smartphone while we're here," Kelly said. "Samuel told me that Flower has started pushing them because they keep the programmers she picked up on Bits busy, and some aliens are using them as a sort of retro fashion statement."

"Even though they won't have a connection anywhere other than Earth?" the president asked in surprise.

"Flower supports them, and you've forgotten that Stryx stations offer connectivity to everything, though whether there will be anybody else on board with a similar device for you to reach is another matter," Kelly said. "My mother used to tell us that smartphones were the center of the universe before the Stryx opened Earth, but when I was a girl, attending school in person and joining clubs were the big things."

"And when I was outside and couldn't get a signal, I remember imagining that the aliens must have technology that kept them connected no matter where they were," Joe said as he thumbed through the menus on the phone Kelly had passed him. "Then I became a mercenary and spent time on Vergallian tech-ban worlds where the fastest communications were messages carried by birds. It's only on space stations and orbitals with mixed populations where the majority of aliens get implants for the sake of the translations."

"But other than the Vergallians, tech-ban worlds are the exception, not the rule," the president said.

"True, and most species carry a device that gives them access to communications and information, but I think they all use them far less than humans," Joe said. "It's all part of the mindset that becoming overly reliant on technology is a slippery slope to extinction."

"The way I see it—Larry must be on his way up," the president interrupted himself after glancing at the vibrating smartphone in his hand.

"Is that an automated alarm system?" Kelly asked.

"Most people on Earth send a text when they arrive in the lobby. It's considered polite."

"Samuel told us that he asked Larry to set up the Human Empire's pavilion for the New World's Fair. I was planning to wait a week or two before going to see him because I imagine he's under a lot of pressure for the opening tomorrow."

"You became the acting president as soon as you sat in that chair," Stephen told her. "If you want to see anybody, you can summon them."

"Does that really work?"

"No, but I thought I'd let you find out for yourself."

"Where will you and Hildy be for the next six months, just in case I have a question?" Kelly asked.

"Around," the president said vaguely. "We aren't leaving Earth unless I accept an invitation from the Dollnick contractor to visit the Venus terraforming project, but Hildy made me promise not to tell you where we're going. If it's really important, you can leave a message," he showed his smartphone again, "and I'll turn it on from time to time to check."

"You don't keep it on all the time?"

"This sabbatical is the only extended vacation I'm going to get until I retire, hopefully when the Human Empire takes over EarthCent," Stephen said. "I need to recharge my own battery. No calls, no texts, no Galactic Free Press. We're going back to nature for six months, but like I said, I'll try to turn the phone on once a week or so to check if you're trying to reach me." He grinned and put the phone back in his pocket. "I won't be offended if I don't hear from you until we return."

"But you will spend a few days getting me up to speed before you go," Kelly said, trying not to sound desperate.

"There's nothing to tell. We leave Earth's governments alone and they leave us alone. The job consists of playing host to alien dignitaries and businessmen visiting Earth, plus the occasional holoconference with our tunnel network ambassadors, all of which you've taken part in since the start."

"But your calendar... Surely you have appointments you'll want to fill me in about."

"They're all with visiting aliens I haven't met yet and will probably never meet in the future, so it's best that you handle them in your own way," Stephen said seriously. "Hildy may be our official director of public relations, but putting a welcoming face on the planet is the president's main job. My one great diplomatic coup was convincing the tunnel network aliens that it was time to start opening businesses on Earth, and that happened while I was visiting Union Station."

"But the—"

A woman in her mid-twenties with a pink spiky hair style stuck her head in the president's office and interrupted with, "Larry, Phil's son to see you. Welcome to Earth, Ambassador McAllister."

"Acting President McAllister," Stephen corrected her. "Kelly, Joe, this is Belladonna. She started working for us last week."

"Belladonna as in the toxic nightshade herb, and everybody calls me Bella," the young woman said. "I told Larry and his wife to wait in the conference room."

"Thank you, Bella," Kelly said. "Do we have anything to offer them?"

"I can make coffee, maybe. Hildy's assistant always took care of the refreshments."

"Coffee, I can manage," the president said. "Why don't you get started, Kelly, and I'll send it in. Come on, Bella. The kitchenette is yours for the next six months. Check with Kelly later about what she wants you to stock for snacks and you can raid petty cash."

"Do you want me to sit in, Kel, or should I go for a walk?" Joe asked.

"You promised to stick with me until Aabina catches up with us," Kelly reminded him. She got up from the desk and followed her husband out of the office. "I was hoping for a little time to settle in, but at least it's just Larry and Georgia." A loud howl of complaint came from the open doors of the conference room, leading EarthCent's acting president to add, "And the male heir."

After the obligatory compliments about how fast the baby was growing, everybody waited while Larry puzzled over connecting his phone to the conference room's projection system. He started a slide show with the biggest circus tent Kelly or Joe had ever seen.

"Your son asked me to come to Earth and take over the Human Empire's exhibition at the World's Fair after he heard through alien channels that their pavilion was a disaster," Larry began. "We were running out of time, and I thought it would look bad to use an alien prefab, but we were able to order the tent from a human-run factory on a Frunge open world."

"Are many of the pavilions prefabs?" Kelly asked.

"I think all the ones set up by alien businesses operating on Earth could be described as prefabricated, though some of them arrived as kits that took a few days to put together. We have the only big tent on the fairgrounds, and most of the city-states or other governments that have pavilions went with some sort of open construction, basically a pole barn or a roof to keep out the rain."

"Everybody knew that they couldn't compete with the aliens on technology, so most of the human pavilions focused on culture," Georgia said as the photographs from Larry's phone flashed by. "There are so many ethnic cuisines on offer that the Galactic Free Press is running a review every day, and I had to share them out with the local freelancers to keep up."

"And a lot of open stages for dance and other performances," Larry said. "The president thought it was important for me to come in and coordinate with you since you'll be escorting all of the visiting alien dignitaries to the fair, and we're hoping that you make our pavilion either the first or the last stop."

"I'm what?" Kelly asked, as Belladonna entered the room carrying a tray with a glass coffee pot, several mismatched mugs, and a circular tin with small cookies separated from one another with crinkly paper cups. "Where's the president?" she continued.

"You're the president now," Belladonna said. "The old one showed me how to make the coffee and left."

"I'm supposed to play tour guide for every diplomatic mission that comes to Earth during the New World's Fair?"

"If you're worried about being on your feet all day, I can let you have a golf cart," Larry said, swiping his phone to stop the slide show after a dozen close-ups of the baby. "The only thing the events management consulting firm the Human Empire hired got right was reserving a pair of golf carts for us. I'm told the whole East Coast has been stripped of them."

"It's not the walking, it's the talking," Kelly said. "What do I know about Earth's cultural achievements? I haven't lived here since I was twenty!"

"The Galactic Free Press has been front-loading all of its fair coverage with articles about the pavilions being prepared by the city-states and legacy nations, because they knew that once the fair opens, the alien businesses and CoSHC pavilions will get all of the attention," Georgia said. "I copied the articles onto this tab for you in case you haven't been following along."

"I didn't realize they were required reading," Kelly said with a sigh, accepting the tab. "If all of the oxygen-breathing tunnel network species send a diplomatic delegation, I'll be at the fair every other week, and then…" She trailed off when she noticed Larry shaking his head. "Just how often am I expected to play tour guide?"

"If you mix and match the business delegations, you might be able to get it down to three days a week," Larry said doubtfully. "Four is probably a safer bet."

"You expect that many alien visitors?"

"Tens of thousands a day. The vast majority of them will be vacationers, but in addition to the diplomatic delegations from the tunnel network species, I expect there will be planetary-level business delegations from all of the open worlds hosting large sovereign human communities."

"But that could run into the dozens," Kelly said in dismay as she unconsciously began rummaging through the cookie tin looking for something that promised a large sugar hit. "Have they all been scheduled?"

Larry shook his head again. "The diplomatic delegations, yes, but the local dignitaries and businessmen from the planets with successful sovereign human communities, no. We assume they'll get in touch with your office as they arrive."

"I need Aabina in this meeting. She went with our luggage to the guest house but she's coming here immediately afterward. Can the two of you wait until she returns?"

"The fair officially opens tomorrow," Georgia reminded the acting president. "They've been letting people in with preview passes the last week, so we think we're ready, but we really should be getting back."

"You can come out and meet us there," Larry suggested. "It wouldn't be a bad idea to get a look around since you'll probably be escorting a group tomorrow. I know that aliens have been arriving all week because they all got preview passes from the president's office. Did he leave you a list?"

"He left me a receptionist they just hired and a drawer full of smartphones," Kelly fumed. "I should have known it was a setup when Libby agreed to all of my conditions without an argument."

Larry and Georgia exchanged a look, and then they both got to their feet. "We have a lunch meeting with some people from the governor-general's office and then we have to get back out to the fairgrounds," Larry said. "We only had time to stop by because the president called us when your ship came out of the tunnel and asked us to come into town a half hour early. Why don't you send out for some food if you haven't eaten, wait for Aabina, and then come out to the fairgrounds to meet us? We should be back at the pavilion in two hours, and there will still be time to show you around some of the major attractions."

"You should loan her one of the guys for the week," Georgia said.

"We can do that. I have two assistants, local university graduates who I hired away from the event planning agency. They're officially working for the Human Empire, and they've met Samuel and Vivian, so they have a pretty good idea of how the whole thing works."

"Then maybe they can explain it to me," Kelly grumbled. "All right, I shouldn't take it out on you."

"That's what I'm here for," Joe said with a grin, standing to accompany the younger couple with the baby stroller to the door. "We'll eat something, regroup, and see you in a few hours."

"I don't know what happened to my manners," Kelly said when he returned. "Maybe I'm still in shock from discovering what I'm really doing on Earth. I can't believe that Stephen dumped this on us and ran. Four days a week of leading alien dignitaries around the fair?"

"You're the most qualified person EarthCent has for the job," Joe told her. "Ever since the Kasilian auction and your interview with Dring, you've been the best-known human ambassador on the tunnel network. And you definitely have the most capable assistant."

"Aabina! I wonder why she's not here yet. Libby, can you ping Aabina and find out if everything is all right? Libby?"

"I think she's only listening in the president's office, and I don't know if the Stryx have the infrastructure in place to ping implants on Earth."

"I'll believe that when Libby tells me herself," Kelly said, taking her smartphone out of her purse. "Let me see if I can remember how these things work." She swiped open the lock screen and groaned as the new-user procedure led her through capturing her photo and fingerprint for security. Then she tapped the microphone icon and spoke in a clear voice, "Call Aabina."

"We haven't given her a phone yet," Joe pointed out.

Kelly let her head hang for a moment, then she ate another cookie and brightened up. "We should order something she'll eat for lunch." She tapped the microphone again and said, "Vergallian Vegan delivery."

"Your location is within the delivery radius of seven Vergallian Vegan restaurants," the phone responded in a tinny voice. "Do you wish to narrow the criteria?"

"Certified by the Council of Queens."

"I don't understand that."

"Displaying the Chef's Chain," Kelly tried again, remembering the official emblem displayed by certified restaurants.

"There is one Vergallian Vegan restaurant matching your search. Downloading the app."

"I thought it would connect a call for you," Joe said.

"That's because you grew up in the sticks," Kelly said. "City restaurants all have an ordering app, and you do the whole thing, including paying, through your phone." A chime sounded and the app for The Student Princess opened. "That was fast. They must have upped the speed again. What do you want, Joe?"

"You know me and vegan. Anything that has some bulk to it is fine."

"They have standard lunches, so I'll just order three different ones and we can share," Kelly said, poking and swiping. "Oh, I take back all of the things I said about Stephen."

"What happened?"

"The phones already have a payment method. I wondered how we were going to get reimbursed for our expenses, but so long as we pay with the phones, it all goes directly to the president's expense account."

Five

"What am I missing?" Myst asked. The young clone stared at the hologram her design station was projecting of the epic set of jewelry she'd designed for the previous season of the professional LARPing league. "Every piece received prominent placement in a quest chain, but Dietro tells me that the first production run of bracelets still hasn't sold out."

"You're looking in the wrong place," Dorothy told her childhood friend. "The problem isn't with your designs, it's with the market. Have you checked the business database? We're paying for the top level now."

"The EarthCent Intelligence subscription Jeeves was complaining about in our last meeting? I don't want to upset him by running up the bill."

"It doesn't work that way. We pay a flat fee for the number of people in the office, and we can use it as much as we want. Hold on a sec." The EarthCent ambassador's daughter saved the sketch of a pantsuit in progress on her oversized Dollnick artist's tab and brought up the interface to the business information database. She navigated rapidly to the retail data, brought up mass-produced jewelry, and did a couple of quick manipulations. "There."

Myst accepted the tab and frowned at the numbers. "Am I supposed to be looking at the gross unit sales for bracelets on Stryx stations? It's in the tens of millions."

"Compare it to rings and necklaces."

"Oh, that's surprising. I knew that rings would be popular because all the species with fingers wear them, but the number of necklaces sold is more than double the number of bracelets. Wow, earrings are even more popular than rings."

"Do you remember last year when Dietro made himself crazy trying to predict how many sets of replica epic jewelry we'd sell based on the LARPing league product placements? Jeeves never said anything about it one way or another, but a few months ago when the inventory for earrings started running low, we found out that he'd cut Dietro's initial order to the manufacturer on Chintoo in half. And even with that, we'll probably end up returning three-quarters of the bracelets for recycling."

"Doesn't that mean there's something wrong with them?" Myst asked. "We never send any dresses or shoes for recycling, and there's always a waiting list for Baa's Bags."

Dorothy shook her head. "It was our first time selling mass-market jewelry, and what Dietro and I didn't realize was that fewer than ten percent of our buyers would go for the whole package. I don't remember the exact numbers, but something like half of our customers only buy one piece of jewelry from the epic set, and then a quarter of them buy two."

"So you're saying that our sales just mirror the numbers for the general categories, and if they weren't buying our jewelry, they'd be buying somebody else's."

"That doesn't mean they don't love your designs," Dorothy said, sensing that the Gem was heading for the wrong conclusion.

"Double negative," Baa commented from the hammock she had strung above Affie's infrequently used workbench in the design room of SBJ Fashions. "If you're going to insist on speaking such a primitive language, you could at least follow the rules."

"The connotation would change if I'd expressed it as a simple positive statement."

"I think I'm ready," Jyndal called from the corner where her workstation was shielded from the rest of the design room by transparent energy fields Jeeves had set up to protect the other employees from mishaps.

"Did you double-check the direction of the enchantment with the right-hand rule?" Baa asked the young woman.

"Twice."

"Then go ahead."

The lights in the room dimmed momentarily, and a few seconds later, Jyndal stepped out of her protected space, beaming as she displayed a fashionable purse. "It didn't shrink away into nothing or catch fire," she said proudly. "The zipper still works, though it's a little warm, and I don't smell anything funny."

"Try dropping something in it, but don't reach inside," the Terragram mage cautioned her apprentice.

"Here," Dorothy said, extending a long plastic ruler that she also used as a straight edge. "You can measure how far it goes without exposing your hand."

Jyndal took the ruler and slowly fed it into the mouth of the purse in a demonstration reminiscent of a sword-swallower in action. It quickly became apparent that the inside dimensions of the purse were now larger than the outside, and Dorothy began to applaud.

"Hold on," Baa said. "Making things disappear is one thing, bringing them back whole is another. Pull it out."

Jyndal's eyes were shining as she drew the ruler out of the purse, but then her face fell, and it was obvious to the observers that something had gone wrong.

"What is it?" Dorothy asked. "The ruler looks fine to me."

"Cursed," Jyndal said. "It's backward."

"I don't understand. What's backward?"

"The numbers," she said, handing it over. "I'm sorry I ruined your ruler."

"Oh, that's okay. I'll use it upside down," Dorothy said, and then gave the girl an impulsive hug. "You did it, almost. We aren't even in LARPing space, and you made a dimensional pocket thingy."

"Thank you for your technical analysis, Mage Crick," Baa said in a voice dripping with sarcasm. She swung her legs out of the hammock and climbed down the short step ladder that she claimed to have found in a recycling bin despite its perfect condition. "Give me the bag, Jyndal." The Terragram mage took the purse from her apprentice, rolled up the loose sleeve of her robe, and plunged her feathered arm up to the elbow in the bag. "Interesting."

"Interesting good?" Jyndal asked hopefully.

"Just interesting," Baa replied, pulling her arm back out with what appeared to be a sandwich wrapped in waxed paper. "Your ability to channel power and affinity for slipping into old ruts continues to surprise me. The bag is indeed cursed, but its dimensional distortion is drifting, meaning with proper guidance, it can be used to filch items from other bags of holding. In some cases, such as a sandwich, a mirror image is just as nutritional as the original."

"I thought that bags-of-holding were supposed to be secure," Dorothy said. "Don't we offer a guarantee?"

"Baa's Bags are secure, but the success of the professional LARPing league has attracted cut-rate products from lower-level mages. Their bags-of-holding use illusions, rather than true pocket dimensions, and are only as secure as the eye of the beholder."

"Is it fixable?" Jyndal asked. "I've been trying to make a bag-of-holding for six months and this is the closest I've come."

"Why would I want to fix it?" Baa asked, reaching into the bag again and this time coming out with a bottle of Union Station Springs water. "At the rate this is going, I'll never have to pay for lunch again."

"You don't need to eat, and it's theft," Dorothy told her. "I thought you agreed not to use your powers to harvest other people's possessions while you're on Union Station."

"What powers? I'm just reaching in Jyndal's cursed bag and groping around." She plunged her arm in a third time and came out with a thick, dog-eared paperback with a bare-chested Dollnick on the cover. "Do you think I would intentionally pick out something like this? I'd need a mirror to read it since all of the words are backward and it opens the wrong way."

"This is exactly what I'm talking about," Jeeves said to Dietro as the two of them entered the design room. The young Stryx launched into a perfect impersonation of the station librarian. "Jeeves, go check on Baa, she's doing something funny. Jeeves, go see how the Human Empire is progressing on the milestones we set. Jeeves, there's a rogue artificial intelligence in—never mind that last one," he interrupted himself in his usual voice, "but you get the point."

"Whine, whine, whine," Baa said. "I was just showing Jyndal that her cursed purse isn't a complete failure. I'll put the sandwich back."

"And the virtual gold? Did you think your sleight-of-hand would go unnoticed?"

"Where there's life, there's hope."

Dietro ignored his quibbling bosses and moved on to Myst's design station where he studied the hologram of the epic set of jewelry. "If that's your new design, it looks too much like the old one," he said. "If we don't get the prototypes over to the League offices this week, the contract will be void, and they can give the product placement to somebody else."

"I finished the new design on the weekend," the young Gem said, waving away the hologram and bringing up a different set of jewelry. "The only piece I'm not sure about is the belly ring, because, you know…"

"Know what?" Dorothy asked.

The clone blushed. "I don't have a belly button."

"I forgot. Can the diamond dangle, or is it strictly for innies?"

"Do you mean that some people have belly buttons that stick out?"

"Sure," Dorothy said. "At least, I've seen them at fashion shows, but not that often. It's not like I spend a lot of time at the beach."

"Have any of you ever heard of moissanite?" Jeeves asked. "It's almost as hard as diamond and has interesting optical properties. There's a low-cost synthesis process that was developed on Earth."

"I thought you could get synthetic diamonds at a price point that worked for the mass-produced pieces," Myst said.

"I was thinking about the originals, for the LARPing league. The Verlock boutique that supplied us with diamonds for the epic set last year didn't see a high enough return on their investment to justify a repeat of the experiment."

"Can't you get somebody else?" Dorothy asked, looking from Jeeves to Dietro. "If we don't use real gems, it's bound to come out, and I can't think of a faster way to kill the Mystique brand."

"I'll go talk to the manager at Volcanic Pipes," Dietro said, not looking very hopeful. "Maybe they misinterpreted the sales data."

"Verlocks misinterpreting data?" Baa scoffed, and then her cat's eyes narrowed. "What if I reached in Jyndal's cursed bag, say while I'm putting the virtual gold back, and happened to find a few hundred carats of natural diamond?"

"I would be sent to my room for the next ten thousand years to write sentences," Jeeves replied. "I imagine Libby would assign me to write, 'I will not allow my business associates to steal,' over and over again on a sheet of synthetic diamond."

"Wow, forced to write sentences on diamond," Dorothy said. "That's poetic justice."

"It's practical justice. If I wrote the sentences on a traditional blackboard, it would wear out every few months and I'd get to take a break."

"The problem with Stryx is that you're no fun," Baa said. "If you aren't going to allow me to use the bag for dimensional fishing, you may as well recover the energy, so Gryph doesn't bill us."

"That's the most sensible idea you've had in ages," Jeeves said, catching the cursed item out of the air with his pincer. The lights in the room brightened for a moment, and then he tossed the purse to Jyndal. "Try again."

"This is the part I don't understand," Dorothy complained. "At first, I thought that Terragram mages used technology to pass as gods with primitive species, but then I found out that the Verlocks have mages, and they certify some humans as being able to tell the future. Then—"

"Predict the future with more accuracy than can be explained by statistics," Baa interjected. "There's a world of difference."

"Then the whole LARPing thing came along, and all of a sudden even I could do magic in LARPing space, as long as I had a teacher or an enchanted item to help."

"Scrolls work too," Dietro said. "I changed myself into a dragon a few weeks ago, but it only lasted for thirty-six minutes."

"Then what happened?" Myst asked.

"I got killed. Next time I'll know not to go sticking my snout into places where I can't survive for ten seconds in my own body."

"This is important," Dorothy said. "I'm trying to get to the bottom of something here. Two years ago, Geb shows up haunting the office next to my mom's embassy before Daniel took it over for CoSHC, and he's some sort of magical familiar."

There was a loud "Mwwrrr!" of objection and a ball of yarn bounced off Dorothy's head.

"And now Jyndal is doing magic outside of a LARPing studio, even if some of her rings end up cursed and her bags-of-holding aren't quite reliable yet. How come the things that only used to work in LARPing space are working in regular space now? Is the space-time continuum breaking down or something?"

"That was quite a speech, even for you," Jeeves said. "Now let me ask you a question. What's the difference between LARPing space and regular space?"

"What do you mean?" Dorothy asked.

"You're going on about the difference between the two, so why don't you tell us what you think that is?"

"But it's obvious. LARPing studios are run by the station librarian, with holographic envelopes superimposed over bots to give a physical presence to the non-player characters. It's all an illusion, except for the bots, the sounds, and I guess Libby uses force fields sometimes."

"Now tell me how that differs from this room," Jeeves said.

"Well, there aren't any, I mean, there are the force fields around Jyndal's work area, and the holograms projected by Myst's design station, but there aren't any bots, other than you," she amended herself. "And Baa just said that cut-rate mages are making illusory bags-of-holding that function in LARPing space, so maybe hers are just better. Is that how it works?" Dorothy asked, her eyebrows knitting together. "Is all magic technical trickery or holographic illusions, but some are better than others?"

"You tell me because I'm not allowed to tell you."

"Believe what you want," Baa said. "There's a reason that all of the so-called advanced species are afraid of me, and it's not because they can't tell a hologram from a hole in a bulkhead."

Dietro cleared his voice and said, "The new designs look good to me, Myst, so print up 3D examples. If the league goes for it, we'll have time to get the originals made and put in an order to Chintoo for mass-market versions. I'm going to be busy the next few weeks with the final push for my show, so anything that anybody would normally bring to me, take it to Dorothy instead."

"How about the problems I would normally bring you?" Dorothy asked.

"Use your judgment. And if you want to know the real score about magic, buy Affie a few drinks and she'll tell you everything we know about it. If you can pry her away from managing affairs for the Alts long enough for a night out, you're doing better than me."

"Vergallians know less about magic than Dollnicks, and that's saying something," Baa scoffed.

"Let's pretend for a minute that I never brought up magic and get back to the part where I'm suddenly in charge of day-to-day business operations," Dorothy said. "If you count all the stitchers we've hired here in the last year, including part-timers, we have over two hundred people working for us just on Union Station. If I have to manage everybody, I'll never get back to ball gowns."

"Finally, a silver lining after all," Jeeves said dryly. "SBJ Fashions has been in business for ten years, so it's time we did a retrospective season. Pick out your favorites and add a few ribbons or new color choices."

"Perfect," Dietro said. "I can promote a tenth-anniversary collection in my sleep, and not introducing a new line will save a tremendous amount of time gearing up to produce it. Baa," he turned back to the Terragram mage. "Have you changed your mind about not letting Jyndal appear on my show? I didn't question it when she was just starting to learn enchantments, but you've been training her for a year now, and the exposure can only help us."

"You and the Grenouthians have had a year to dig up contestants with magical talent," Baa countered. "Those advertisements the bunnies have been running at fantasy cons should have brought the little witches out of the shadows."

"We have plenty of talent lined up, but other than the Verlocks, they're largely untrained. We've got a Frunge who can accelerate plant growth, a Dollnick who can bend copper pipes without touching them, and a Grenouthian who can make herself appear in recorded video when she wasn't present."

"If I was the only vote on the panel, she'd win."

"I thought you categorically refused to be on the panel of judges," Dietro said.

"I told you that I've got better things to do with my time than to watch a bunch of talentless hacks trying to bend spoons with their minds or guess what playing card somebody is looking at. If you can get some real talent, I'll reconsider, but a Frunge plant-talker and a Dollnick plumber with an overactive imagination don't make the cut. A Grenouthian who can insert herself into digital recordings—that would be interesting if it's true."

"It's not," Jeeves said. "I would have heard about it by now if it was."

"Anybody else?" Baa asked Dietro.

"I thought the plant talker—"

"Time-lapse photography," Jeeves interrupted.

"And the pipe bender—" Dietro paused to see if the young Stryx would shoot the Dollnick down as well, "—were talented, and we need good visuals for the audience. The problem with putting on a Verlock who can create minor enchantments of protection for Live Action Role Playing is that we can't show it happening."

"The number one sign of a charlatan is that they can't make their magic happen if somebody is watching," Baa told him. "Real mages love an audience."

"It's not that the Verlock mages can't work with an audience, it's that there's nothing to see. A cloak that's been enchanted to give plus one protection from arrows looks just like a regular cloak."

"Not to me or Geb."

Six

"...which is how mammalian ruminants came to form the staple of the Frunge diet," Czeros concluded.

The two women stared at the Frunge ambassador with expressions of disbelief. Ofer came out of Aabina's office, which he had taken over while the Vergallian was on Earth with Kelly, and cleared his throat.

"Is it important, Consul?" Judith asked Ofer. "The Gem ambassador is coming to help us set up this afternoon's taste tests for new *All Species Cookbook* recipes and the embassy lobby is going to be a madhouse."

"I just wanted to tell you that I'm going to the casino with Daniel and I won't be back today."

"Ambassador McAllister hasn't even been gone two weeks and you're already gambling during work hours?" Czeros asked. "I'm impressed."

"It is work, or at least, Daniel says it is," Ofer explained. "We're meeting the Thark ambassador about the new commission and—"

"Say no more," the Frunge ambassador interrupted as he began backing towards the exit. "I have urgent work waiting in my embassy that will keep me busy for at least the next four hours on your clock. My apologies, ladies, but we can pick this up another time."

"Was it something I said?" Ofer asked as the doors slid closed behind Czeros.

"I've been working in the embassy less than a month," Judith reminded her nominal boss. "You tell me."

The consul thought for a moment. "I probably shouldn't have mentioned the new commission without finding out whether Ambassador Czeros has been appointed to a leadership role," he eventually said. "If the Stryx hear him express an interest, he might get drafted into serving."

"Daniel told me not to wait dinner on him tonight because the Gambling Commission is meeting again," Shaina said. "I swear he's enjoying these casino site visits a little too much. He used to have a gambling problem before we married."

"How did you get him to stop?" Judith asked the older woman.

"I didn't, work did. Gambling properly is a full-time occupation."

"But it's just chance," Ofer protested. "Even I know that casino games are all designed so that the house rakes in a steady percentage. If somebody gambled full-time, they would inevitably lose all their money."

"Daniel's gambling problem was that he was good enough to win, but it's slow, grinding work," Shaina explained. "And professional gamblers don't play against the house, at least, not in modern casinos." She looked up at the tall young man, trying to read his face. "I know you're good at math and you have an excellent memory, but don't confuse the challenge of beating other players with constructive employment. Ultimately, whether you win or lose, gambling is a terribly wasteful method of creating economic activity."

"Then why do the Stryx allow it on their stations?"

"They aren't vice cops, and you can't stop sentients from gambling. It's not uncommon for artificial people and other artificial intelligences to get hooked for stretches of time."

"But who would play against them?" Ofer asked. "With perfect memories and computational skills, the odds will always be in their favor."

"You're forgetting the element of luck and the art of the bluff," Shaina told him. "Just remember that gamblers keep even weirder hours than diplomats, and your girlfriend wouldn't like it."

"Jyndal doesn't sleep as much as me, and according to Baa, eventually she won't have to sleep at all. I just hope she has her breakthrough so we can get married before I'm too old. Her aging is supposed to slow down as well."

"I thought that was all worked out," Judith said with a frown. "You and Jyndal are coming to our apartment for a meal on Friday, and you're going to babysit while Bob takes me to a Grenouthian press event."

"We are?" Ofer asked.

"When's the last time Jyndal spent any time around children? When she was one herself?"

"I think Dorothy still brings Richard to work some days, though Jyndal told me he mainly stays in the nursery. But we'll have to ask Baa."

"Baa, Baa, Baa," Judith said dismissively. "It's like listening to a sheep."

Shaina's sister Brinda entered the embassy lobby from the conference room. "The Thark ambassador has arrived, so Daniel is waiting for you, Ofer," she said. "And I just got a weird message for you from an unidentified sender saying that Friday evening is fine but don't make a habit of it."

"You see?" Ofer said to Judith. "Baa knows everything."

"I'll check with EarthCent Intelligence who they're using to sweep for bugs these days," the new embassy manager said. "We'll be here all afternoon working on the cookbook if you or Daniel need anything. If you gamble, use your own money. I won't refund you from petty cash."

Ofer crossed through the conference room into CoSHC's shared workspace and found Daniel crouched next to the Thark ambassador who was throwing dice off the wall.

"Boxcars," the cheerful alien declared when both dice came to rest with six pips showing. "It's all in the wrist."

"I thought we were going to the casino to calibrate the games," Daniel said. "Why would you bring loaded dice?"

"Just because the games are honest doesn't mean that the players are honest. Supervising a casino also means making sure that they're putting in the effort to catch cheats. Both of us are known, but your consul is a new face."

"You want me to try to cheat in the casino?" Ofer asked, his voice rising. "I've never cheated at anything in my life."

"Then you should consider this a valuable opportunity," the Thark ambassador said, handing over the dice. "These are exact replicas of official issue used in the casino for Human craps games."

"Do I have to do this?" Ofer asked Daniel. "I don't think I'd be any good at it. I'm nervous enough just being in crowds."

"The ambassador was kidding," Daniel said. "He wouldn't ask you to test a game without practicing first."

"I didn't mean today," the Thark said, though the translation generated by the diplomatic implants imparted a tone of disappointment. "Take these and work on throwing boxcars. When you can make them come up three times in a row, you're ready."

"Shouldn't he be able to make clean rolls as well?"

"I thought that was implied."

"But if I go to the casino with the two of you today, won't that make me your known associate?" Ofer asked.

"True, I didn't think of that," the Thark said, mainly because he had been expecting the consul to jump on the opportunity to have some fun. "Are you sure you don't want to just give it a try?"

"I'm sure."

The alien ambassador held out his hand. "Then I suppose you may as well return them." Something occurred to him just as he was about to put the dice in his pocket, and he asked, "Have they explained to you about diplomatic immunity?"

"I know what it is in theory," Ofer said. "It can't apply to cheating in casinos, though. Can it?"

"You could be the test case."

"Or not," Daniel said, putting one hand on the tall young man's shoulder, the other on the short Thark's, and guiding them both towards the door. "The reason I asked Ofer to accompany us today is that he's never had occasion to make any sort of site inspection. He'll soon be called upon to do so while filling in for some of Ambassador McAllister's obligations."

"Which ones are you sticking him with?" the alien ambassador asked.

"To start with, the Gaming Rules Committee. Kelly has been on it ever since she came to Union Station, and she even fills in for Ortha as chair if he's on vacation."

"Isn't gaming just another word for gambling?" Ofer asked.

"Maybe on Earth," the Thark ambassador said. "The Gaming Rules Committee deals primarily with tournament play for games of strategy, though they've recently been spending most of their time moderating disputes about the Professional LARPing League."

"Are you a member of the committee?"

"Technically, but I only get to one in ten meetings, and that's if I'm not traveling."

"And the Stryx let you get away with it?" Daniel asked in surprise.

"As long as they have a quorum, nobody complains, and since the younger species are all obsessed with gaming, they always have a quorum," the Thark said as they entered the lift tube. "Ortha records the meetings for me, and I listen to them if I have trouble sleeping. Camelot, please."

"The customer entrance or the security room?" the station librarian inquired.

"Customer entrance, unless one of you has a preference."

"We'll start on the casino floor, and we can always go up afterward," Daniel said, and the lift tube capsule began to move. "So, are you saying that if I can't make one of your Gambling Commission meetings at three in the morning you won't hold it against me?"

The Thark ambassador chuckled. "I'm not Ortha, and something tells me you haven't been catching up with the minutes from Void Station."

"Is that where the Gambling Commission was sitting before it moved here? I didn't know I was supposed to dig into the past. How far back do the records go?"

"For the Gambling Commission? Before the Frunge and the Dollnicks joined the tunnel network, so a couple of million years. The Stryx are very good at recordkeeping."

"So how far back are new commission members required to read?" Daniel asked, not hiding the dread in his voice.

"There's no requirement at all," the Thark said. "But it's a good idea to look back a few meetings whenever a commission moves to try to figure out why the previous members were so anxious to see it transferred into somebody else's jurisdiction."

"The commissions don't move according to a predetermined schedule?" Ofer asked as they exited the lift tube in front of the gaudy entrance to the Camelot Casino.

"Some do, some don't. The Gambling Commission is generally considered a plum assignment because the site visits tend to be at vacation resorts. When I reviewed the minutes from Void Station—but we shouldn't discuss it in public," the alien cut himself short as they entered the casino.

"If you don't give me a hint, I'm going to end up getting the minutes from Libby and trying to read them on my heads-up display while we're walking around," Daniel said.

"Humans."

"That's the whole hint? Humans?"

"If I tell you the whole thing it's not a hint," the Thark ambassador said as he handed Ofer a programmable cred. "Take this to the cashier and ask for a large tray."

"Shouldn't I use my own programmable cred?" the consul asked.

"A large tray is one hundred thousand creds in chips. Do you have that much saved?"

"Maybe in another forty years," Ofer said. "I'll be right back."

"All right, you got rid of him," Daniel said. "What does humanity have to do with the Gambling Commission moving to Union Station."

The Thark ambassador sighed and motioned for Daniel to follow him over to a privacy booth. Once they entered, the alien tapped the stone of what looked like a class ring, which despite its similarity to a ruby, began to glow blue.

"Human Empire," the alien said, hiding his mouth with his hand in case there were lip readers who spoke Thark lurking about. "They want to start a multi-world lottery."

"I remember hearing something about that, but I didn't give it a second thought," Daniel said. "What could be simpler than a lottery? Does the tunnel network treaty have requirements about the chance of winning?"

"Not the tunnel network, every individual species. The issue isn't with establishing a lottery that operates on Earth or the Stryx stations. The problem is that over half of humanity lives on planets belonging to other species."

"How does moving the commission here make establishing the lottery any less complicated?"

The Thark ambassador laughed. "For the former commissioners on Void Station, the level of complication just went to zero."

"And now it's our problem," Daniel said, nodding as the alien's meaning sank in. He spied Ofer threading his way towards them through the gaming tables with a large tray of casino chips slotted into holders. "He looks confused, so we better get out there. If you can send me the relevant minutes, I'll read them before the next meeting."

"A woman I've never met before in my life just asked me if I wanted to see her room," Ofer reported to Daniel as soon as he joined the ambassadors. "Is looking at furniture part of making site visits?"

"It may be for Humans," the Thark ambassador said. "I'm only interested in the gambling tables."

"She wasn't talking about showing you the furniture," Daniel told the naïve consul.

"What else is there to see in a hotel?" Ofer asked. "It's not like there are balconies in space."

"I've been to resort orbitals with balconies, though they're glassed over as a backup to the atmosphere retention field, or perhaps it's the other way around," the Thark told the young man while relieving him of the tray. "What I think Associate Ambassador Cohan was trying to express was that the individual in question was more interested in my chips than your conversation."

"I didn't say a word to her before she invited me to her room, so I guess that makes sense."

"She was probably a professional," Daniel added. "The casino licenses escorts to keep them honest."

"A large tray would tempt many professionals astray," the alien said. "Take all of the yellows, Ofer. They're only ten creds each. Daniel, you take the reds, which are hundreds, and I'll gamble the blues, which are thousands. We can meet at the bar in three hours to tally up."

"I thought we'd stick together," Daniel said. "I suspect Ofer wouldn't be comfortable gambling with your money, and I'd like to see how you go about testing the tables."

"We'll get a third as much done sticking together, but if you insist," the Thark ambassador said. "I had a report of problems on the Vergallian Royals table. Have you played?"

"It's basically poker, but there are a hundred cards in the deck with ten suits of ten cards."

"So you haven't."

Daniel shrugged. "That's what it looked like from a distance. I stick with games I know in casinos."

"You can both stand behind me, but under no circumstances touch my cards or my chips or I'll forfeit the hand," the Thark ambassador said. "And if you find yourselves tempted to look at another player's hand and transmit that information to me by, say, a numeric tapping code on my shoulder..."

"He's joking," Daniel told the horrified-looking Ofer. "We'll just observe, and if you get bored, I'll show you around the games that I know."

Three hours later, the Thark rose from the table exactly fifty creds ahead, which he slid to the dealer as a tip. He motioned for Ofer to pick up the tray which looked like it had just come from the cashier's cage. "Take that back and get this refilled," he said, placing his programmable cred on top.

"Impressive," Daniel said to the alien ambassador as the young man hurried off. "I thought you were going to come away a big winner, but you managed to winnow down perfectly."

"It adds a little excitement to the otherwise dreary job of ensuring that the dealers aren't cheating," the Thark said. "The players didn't offer much competition, aside from the young princess who looks like she ran away from the palace to escape from royal training."

"I wondered if she was old enough to be playing, but she does nothing but win."

"If she were older, I'd suspect her of cheating with her pheromones, but watching her play, it's clear she's an expert. She probably had a tutor who was obsessed with the game and passed it on to her. In any case, she's the station management's problem, not ours."

"Why should she be anybody's problem?" Daniel asked.

"Did you see any bodyguards around?"

"Now that you mention it, she seemed to be alone."

"She's part of somebody's line of succession, I could tell that much just by watching her play," the Thark ambassador said. "If she was here on vacation, she'd at least be accompanied by a companion and a few guards. Definitely a runner."

"And the Stryx will send her back?"

"That's where the problem comes in. They have a soft spot for underage runaways from all species, but when it comes to Vergallian royals, there are treaty—look. Jeeves is floating over to have a word with her."

Daniel glanced back towards the table and saw that the young Stryx had indeed approached the apparent runaway. The beautiful young princess kept her composure, nodded a few times, gathered her chips, and followed the floating robot away from the table.

"I wonder where he's bringing her?"

"Vergallian embassy would be my guess. The Stryx won't let the ambassador take the girl into custody, but it's best that all parties know where they stand."

"Here's your programmable cred," Ofer said. "I checked the balance and it went back up by a hundred thousand."

"And you aren't going to seek my financial advice?" the Thark ambassador asked. "That's the usual reaction of Humans who see it."

"Why don't you hide the balance?" Daniel asked.

"Away from Stryx stations, I sometimes do, but I enjoy taking questions from prim—from Humans," the alien corrected himself. "I usually learn more from your questions than you do from my answers."

"I have lots of questions," Ofer said. "Most people say I have too many."

"Then we should get along just fine. But now I have to go to the off-world betting facility for the meeting, and as chairman, I should be at least ten minutes early. Will you be accompanying us?"

The young man shot Daniel a guilty look, and the associate ambassador said. "Go and see Jyndal if you have a date. I have to be at the meeting whether or not you come." After Ofer took his leave of the Thark ambassador and hurried off, Daniel said, "I don't remember ever being that young."

"But it was only a couple of decades ago," the alien pointed out as they headed for the lift tube.

"We have selective memories. It's a trait of the species."

"That could explain some of the deficits in analytical thinking I've observed among the Human members of my investing club," the Thark said. "Those who forget their mistakes can't learn from them."

"Are you comfortable talking in here?" Daniel asked as they entered the lift tube capsule.

"Off-world betting parlor, and yes, the lift tubes are the safest place on the station."

"So is the Human Empire's lottery scheme undoable, or will they just have to jump through a lot of hoops with the governments of open worlds and planets with contract laborers."

"It's not just hoops, it's revenue sharing," the Thark ambassador explained. "No species in the galaxy is going to let a foreign government come in and run a lottery in their territory. It's a form of tax, you know."

"That sounds right, but when Samuel mentioned the idea to me, he didn't seem aware of the difficulties," Daniel said. "He told me it came up while they were brainstorming revenue-generating ideas with students at their school of government."

"Then establishing a lottery may be more valuable as an educational experience than as a profit center. They'll certainly get a lot of practice negotiating, given the hundreds of worlds and orbitals involved."

"It wouldn't be one agreement with each species?"

The Thark shook his head. "Lotteries are always handled at the local government level, it's like a sacred privilege. Some planets may even have different lottery authorities for every continent or regional administration." The lift tube doors slid open and the alien concluded, "We'll talk about it in the meeting if we have time after the election."

"What election?" Daniel asked. "I didn't see any announcement."

"Commissions always hold an election for officers in a public meeting. We'll try to make a show of competing for positions even though nobody wants the extra responsibilities. I took the liberty of putting your name in for secretary."

Seven

EarthCent's acting president kept a hold of her husband's elbow as they descended the stairs from the monorail station, and she silently thanked Aabina for talking her into wearing comfortable walking shoes.

"I saw an elevator on the platform," Joe said as they paused on a landing. "Maybe we should take it next time."

"And tell the group of dignitaries that we're escorting to meet us at the bottom?" Kelly asked. "If the delegation from the Verlock Empire hadn't postponed due to volcanic activity on their homeworld, we would have been leading the emperor's grandson and his entourage today."

"If you're going to worry about appearances, we can forget about leading the tours in Larry's golf cart."

"I know. I'm just hoping that we can minimize the number of hours we spend on our feet by carefully planning our route and including a lot of cultural activities where we sit and watch what's happening on the stage."

"Good plan," Joe said as they started down the second flight of stairs. "What you'll want to avoid is going into some of the larger pavilions with industrial exhibits where everybody is expected to stand and watch."

"I'm hoping that none of our guests will be interested in those," Kelly said. "The advanced species are already familiar with each other's technology, so the pavilions set up by the alien businesses operating on Earth and the sovereign human communities from open worlds will draw their visitors from the local population. I plan to take the visiting dignitaries to the exhibits put on by ethnic groups from around the world and end at the Human Empire pavilion."

"I suppose the aliens do find our lack of cultural standardization fascinating. I remember how surprised Ambassador Bork was when he found out that there are still thousands of languages spoken on Earth and that Humanese is just English with a lot of borrowed words creeping in."

"And Hortens who haven't met Humans are always excited by our different skin colors. The only other species with so much variety in their coloration is the Grenouthians, and between you and me, I think some of the females dye their fur."

As they stepped onto the crowded plaza at the foot of the stairs, Joe felt a strange pins-and-needles feeling in his upper left leg, and for a moment he wondered if it was the first sign of a heart attack. Then he remembered changing the smartphone ringer to vibrate and pulled the offending device out of his pocket. "Hello?"

"Morning, Joe," Larry's voice blared out of the phone's speaker. "I saw the two of you come down the stairs. I'm waiting with the cart just past the turnstiles at the far left. If you come around that way, I can open the gate and save you from waiting in line."

"It's on speaker," Kelly hissed at Joe as a number of people looked over to see who was getting special treatment.

"How come the old fogies get to go ahead of everybody?" a teenager whined to his mother. "It's not like they're celebrities or we'd know them."

"Maybe they were somebody years ago and we just don't recognize them now," the woman said, not bothering to lower her voice. "Look at those lines. We preregistered a month ago and it's still going to take fifteen minutes to get in."

"I'm definitely taking the gate now," Kelly said, and she began to skirt the crowd to the left. "Maybe I should get a hat with 'Acting President' embroidered on the front."

"If you do, I'm staying home," Joe said with a laugh. "Can you even imagine how many complaints you'd get if people knew who you were?"

"Most of them have probably forgotten that EarthCent even exists, if they ever knew. I've been watching the local news since we got here and it hasn't come up even once."

"You know, we better get Larry to introduce us to the management while we're here so we can take the alien dignitaries through the gate. I don't think their security details would be happy with the idea of standing in line with a crowd."

When they reached the gate, which was attached to a glassed-in guard booth, Larry was waiting out front with a uniformed woman in her forties who was laughing so hard that tears were coming from her eyes. A large Huktra was standing with them, looking rather pleased with himself that his joke had gone over so well.

"President McAllister, Joe," Larry greeted them. "This is Colonel Davidson from the New York Guard who is managing fair security, and Myort, the cultural attaché from the Huktra embassy who is the officer of the day in charge of the onsite fraud brigade from the tunnel network species."

"Colonel," Kelly said, shaking hands with the woman who was trying desperately to regain her composure. She cocked her head a little when looking at the alien as if his appearance rang a vague bell. "Have we met before, Myort?"

"A long time ago, and I doubt you'd remember," the Huktra said. "I'm sure you and the colonel have much to discuss, and I don't want to intrude on your time, but I asked Larry to introduce me so we could exchange our information in case you need to get in touch." The dragon-like alien fished a smartphone out of his pouch and held it out toward Kelly.

"I'm supposed to do something?" she asked, glancing at her husband.

"It must be the sharing function Aabina told us about," Joe said. "Try holding your phone up against his."

"That's right," Myort encouraged her. "You'll get an on-screen prompt asking you to authorize sharing information, and then we'll be on each other's certified contacts list."

Kelly followed the instructions, and her phone rewarded her with a happy beep. Then the alien extended his phone towards Joe, who duplicated the procedure.

"Look at your contact list," the acting president said to her husband. "There's an animated dragon hovering next to Myort's number."

"You can buy custom contact avatars from the programmers working the phone kiosks in the Human Empire pavilion," Myort told them. "I'll leave you to get acquainted with the colonel, and you're all invited to a reception at the Huktra embassy in two months when the official delegation from our empire arrives. I'll be in contact," he concluded, giving his smartphone a shake before returning it to his pouch and hurrying off.

"Pam," Colonel Davidson reintroduced herself once Myort was gone. "He always has a joke when he comes to see me, which is as good as saying he's up to something. But we have strict orders from the governor-general not to interfere with the alien intelligence agents unless it's in response to an explicit complaint. They've been given a free hand to police frauds targeting alien guests on the fairgrounds, which to be honest, makes our job a lot easier."

"Over the next six months, President McAllister will be escorting official delegations to the fair several days a week," Larry told the colonel. "The diplomatic delegations, and perhaps some of the other dignitaries, may be accompanied by security, media, and family members, making for a large entourage. The governor-general's office cooperates with EarthCent and has provided special passes, but I'm hoping you can update all of the Guard personnel working on-site to avoid potential misunderstandings."

"Of course," Pam said, and producing her smartphone, took pictures of Kelly and Joe, both individually and together. "Will there be anybody else in regular attendance?"

"My special assistant, Aabina," Kelly said. "She'll be meeting us here at lunch, but she had an appointment at the Vergallian embassy this morning."

"Another one of those Ladies in Waiting who wants to become Vergallian? We've been seeing more of that in the Guard in the last year or two."

Kelly shook her head and thumbed through the folder of videos she'd taken for practice. She found one of her special assistant doing Vergallian stretching exercises in the morning and showed it to the colonel. "This is her."

Pam's eyes widened. "How did you ever get an upper-caste Vergallian to work as your assistant? She looks like a princess from a drama."

"Aabina *is* a princess. She started working for my embassy as a co-op student sent by the Open University and stayed on for the experience."

"Do you mind if I copy this?" The colonel brought her phone close to Kelly's, and the acting president read the prompt requesting a screen copy before hitting the confirmation. "I'll send a special text to all of the Guard personnel with the pictures I just took, plus this one, so they'll all recognize you."

"They'll recognize Aabina, anyway," Joe said with a laugh. "I'm not that photogenic."

"Will you require a security detail on the fairgrounds?" Pam followed up. "I'm not exactly overstaffed, but I do have some roving patrols just showing the flag, and I could assign one of them to you while you're on the grounds."

"We'll only be here when we're accompanying alien delegations, and they'll almost certainly have their own security," Kelly said.

"And they all know how to take care of themselves," Joe added. "I worked some security details as a mercenary when I was young, and the Vergallian royals hired us more for the sake of the pageantry of employing aliens than for our effectiveness. The tunnel network species all treat training in unarmed combat as part of physical education for youth."

"That explains it," the colonel said, nodding her head. "This is the first assignment I've been on where people approach me to turn themselves in for attempted pick-pocketing, and several of them were sporting broken wrists. It seems that some alien tourists fail to see the humor in attempted larceny."

"Will New York prosecute any of the tourists for using excessive force?"

Pam shook her head again. "We're supposed to use our judgment, but the tenor of our orders is not to cause any diplomatic incidents unless absolutely necessary. From what I've seen so far, the aliens are a well-behaved lot if you don't poke them with pointy sticks."

"That's as good a description as I've heard," Joe said, laughing again. "Have you been through the pavilions of the local alien businesses? We're going to focus on human accomplishments when we're taking the dignitaries around, so this morning is our chance to be tourists."

"Have you ever seen Frunge wing sets in action? There's a pavilion sponsored by an industrial cooperative from Asia that's showing off all sorts of Frunge technology and textiles manufactured under license. Believe it or not, they even have an old-fashioned blacksmith demonstrating how to forge swords."

"I've tried the wings on vacation a few times, and the Frunge are crazy about metal working."

"Are any of the Grenouthian reserves putting on reenactments?" Kelly asked. "I'm hoping that we'll have time to visit a few of them while we're on Earth, but just in case we don't make it, an exhibition could give us a taste of what we're missing."

"I can recommend the castle," Pam said. "It's from the Grenouthian reserve in Bavaria, and rather than disassembling it stone by stone and rebuilding it on site, they brought in a terraforming ship with the power to scoop up the whole thing and bring it here. I'm told they built a roof over the hole it made so they'll be able to return the castle with its foundations and all when the fair is over."

"That sounds good, Joe. And you like Bavarian beer."

"I'll fall asleep if I drink more than a single sample size," Joe said, but he listened as the colonel gave them instructions for reaching the pavilion. Then he and Kelly joined Larry at the golf cart, where the Human Empire's Minister of Trade explained the basic operation of the electric vehicle.

"Why doesn't it float?" Kelly asked.

"They have floater versions, I suppose, but I'm told that millions of these were manufactured for retirement communities a century ago, and it's still cheaper to keep them running by cannibalizing parts than to replace them."

"Seems pretty straightforward," Joe said. "Electric motor, battery, steer with the front wheels."

"The governor is limited to roughly twice normal walking speed during fair hours, and collision avoidance technology initiates deceleration any time you get within two cart-lengths of something directly in front of you," Larry warned them. "If you try to follow people closer than that, at one cart-length it matches speed with whatever is in front of you, regardless of how hard you press on the accelerator."

"Sounds like the voice of experience."

"What good are safety features if you don't test them?" Larry asked with a grin. "At any rate, here's the key tab. The cart won't go anywhere if it's not within arm's length of the steering wheel."

"Do I have to wear it on my wrist?" Joe asked, accepting the elastic band with the plastic-encased transponder.

"I do it that way because it's convenient. Your pocket may be close enough, but the president's purse will be too far if she's in the passenger seat."

"Acting president," Kelly corrected him. "Thank you for all of the help, and we'll see you at the Human Empire pavilion tomorrow afternoon when we bring the Drazen delegation."

The silk pennants flying from the towers of the imported castle soon came into view, though navigating the golf cart through the crowds of fair visitors proved to be almost more bother than it was worth. In the end, Joe wasn't sure it had saved them any time at all, but at least they had been sitting rather than on their feet.

"Look, Joe," Kelly cried, pointing at one of the pushcarts parked near the castle's entrance. "It's like a sign from heaven."

"Organic memory supplements?" Joe read the sign doubtfully.

"Ginkgo biloba, I've heard of that," she said, getting out of their ride and making a beeline for the pushcart with its tastefully displayed tapestry featuring the Chinese tree. "Excuse me, Miss. Is your memory supplement really organic?"

"And certified by the Organic Supplements Council," the young woman said, pointing at a framed certificate. "The supplements sold in supermarkets are often bulked up with other so-called medicinal herbs, but ours is guaranteed one-hundred percent organic ginkgo biloba."

"Is it guaranteed to work?" Joe asked from the golfcart.

"I can show you testimonials from hundreds of happy users. We also have a line of fish oil capsules that boost your general brain functioning."

"I could use that too," the acting president said happily. "How much are they?"

"We're offering a special Brain Care package that includes the ginkgo, the fish oil, and ginseng, all for thirty eBucks. They'd cost you fifteen eBucks each if they were sold separately, and they come with this book of math puzzles that will improve your cognitive function and problem-solving ability."

"That last part I can believe," Joe said, reaching for his new wallet and extracting a few notes.

The young woman's nose crinkled as if she'd smelled something bad. "Are they still exchanging creds into paper eBucks for tourists? It kind of defeats the whole purpose, don't you think?"

"But do you take them?"

"I can give you an additional ten percent off if you pay with your phones."

"Cash is king," Joe said, passing over the paper bills.

"How old are these?" the young woman asked doubtfully, holding them up to the sun and squinting. "This one doesn't even have the space elevator in the water mark." She returned the ten eBuck note and held up the next one. "What is that?"

Joe took it back and squinted against the sun. "It's a whale, I think. Or maybe a dolphin?"

"Oh, right. Dolphin Dollars, I've heard of those." She accepted the bill, and instead of putting it in the cash box, placed it to the side and made up the difference with a payment from her phone. "I think I'll hold onto it to show my friends."

Kelly happily loaded her purse with the three bottles of supplements and the puzzle book before asking Joe,

"Where did you get the paper money? I thought we were going to use our phones to pay for everything."

"I've got a few thousand eBucks worth that I've accepted in payment from down-on-their-luck traders over the years," Joe said. "The value hasn't fallen all that much versus the Stryx cred, so I think there's an implicit link."

"You never asked at EarthCent Intelligence?"

"I didn't see the point. I knew we'd get back to Earth eventually and I thought it was a good way of saving for a vacation."

"So we have to spend it all while we're here," Kelly said in a tone that her husband knew meant that the money was as good as gone.

"Looks like the castle is emptying out," Joe said, watching as a flood of fairgoers emerged through the castle gatehouse, some of them hurrying through the exit with a fearful glance up at the massive portcullis suspended overhead. "I bet that means they just finished a staged demonstration and there won't be another one for a while."

"I wish the New World's Fair supported the standard information channel for implants."

"Did you check? Hang on, there is one," Joe said, staring off into space with a near-sighted gaze that indicated he was reading something on his heads-up display. "It says that the information channel is being broadcast and updated thanks to a generous donation from Drazen Foods." He was silent for a moment while navigating with eye movements, and then continued, "We just missed a medieval dueling reenactment and the next one is at noon."

"That's no good, we're meeting Aabina for lunch," Kelly said. "Check if there are any traditional makers of children's toys."

"There are some hits for toy makers in the standard directory but none in the castle. I thought you were interested in getting a taste of a Grenouthian reenactment preserve in case we don't get to one."

"That was before they took the rest of the morning off. If I want to look at medieval weapons on the wall, I can always visit Bork's office. Now I'm shopping."

"For children's toys," Joe said, wanting to make sure he was following his wife's thought process.

"But not any toys, traditional Earth toys. Maybe something made from wood."

"Then this is your lucky day because I just found the location of Toymaker's Row. Do you want to walk or take the golf cart?"

"How far is it?"

"Hold on a second," Joe said, closing one eye and holding his hand up in front of the other eye with the thumb and forefinger spread apart. "If I can just transfer that to the scale, no, wait. There's a measurement tool in the menu. It's six minutes walking."

"Then let's leave the cart here," Kelly said. "The castle will make it easy to find. Did they give the distance in minutes?"

"I sure hope they're talking about walking time and not longitude, because if my memory is correct, that would be close to seven miles."

"You don't have to show off that your memory is better than mine, and with my ginkgo biloba, ginseng, and fish oil, I intend to give you a run for your money."

"You're forgetting the math puzzles."

"I didn't buy those, they were just a throw-in," Kelly said as she took Joe's arm again. "Are you keeping the map overlay live on your heads-up display? I could never do that without getting dizzy."

"Nice to know I'm still good for something. Which one of the grandkids are you shopping for?"

"All of them. We don't have to buy everything today, but I don't want to leave it for the last minute either. Plus, anything we buy early we can send back to Union Station in the diplomatic pouch rather than carrying it in our baggage."

Eight

"I can't believe I'm meeting my friends for drinks at seven in the morning," Dorothy said. "If Richard was awake, he'd be shocked."

"Are two-year-old Humans so judgmental?" Flazint asked, her hair vines rustling with humor. "Frunge drinking gardens are supposed to be places to relax and have quiet conversations, and on our clock, these are the prime evening hours. I'm almost surprised the owner found room for us."

"I noticed an acoustic isolation field kicking in when we entered the grove. I think they're worried that Richard will wake up and start screaming."

"I didn't want to bring it up in case you took offense, and I'm surprised that you noticed."

"I set my implant to beep whenever I enter or exit an acoustic isolation field," the EarthCent ambassador's daughter explained. "It's a trick that Dietro showed me."

"I've missed seeing everybody at work, but we only have the big family reunions every fifty years or so," Flazint said. "It was fun getting to know all of the little shrubs I've never met, but it's good to be back on Union Station, and I'm really looking forward to working again. What did I miss?"

"Jyndal's enchantments have improved to the point that she's not accidentally cursing enough rings to meet the demand for them, so Baa is stuck making up the difference. And the Professional LARPing League approved Myst's new epic set of jewelry for the new season, so Jeeves took the designs to Chintoo to contract for production of the consumer versions."

"Jeeves went himself?"

"It's funny," Dorothy said. "Since Shaina and Brinda stepped back from the business, Jeeves is putting more and more responsibility on me and Dietro, but at the same time, he's getting more pincer-on about the production side."

"Between the nanofabric fitting franchises, and all the bespoke orders we're sending to Flower Apparel, our sales must be up by an order of magnitude over a couple of years ago," Flazint said. "That's serious money for a young Stryx."

"Maybe. He's not coming into the office as much, but he knows everything that happens, which is kind of annoying."

"And how's Affie?"

"Other than being late?" Dorothy checked the time on her implant and backtracked. "Alright, she's still got two minutes, but your guess is as good as mine. She comes by the office a couple of times a week to see Dietro, but I captured an image of the mess on her workbench last month and nothing has moved since then. When she's not busy substitute queening for the Alts, Ambassador Aleeytis has her filling in at the Vergallian embassy."

"A princess is too precious a resource to waste," Flazint quoted the old Vergallian saying. "It was probably inevitable that they would get her in harness one way or another."

"Shush, here she comes."

"Welcome back, Flaz," Affie said as she entered the grove. "Have you been to see Tzachan yet?"

"He was waiting for me at the travel concourse when I arrived," the Frunge girl said, and the chlorophyll darkened her hair vines as she hastened to add, "It doesn't count as a date because I was traveling unescorted."

"We've been seeing a lot of him at the office lately because of the intellectual property issues related to the new jewelry," Dorothy said. "Jeeves grumbles about the bills, but my mom says that it's better to spend money on legal advice up front and not get dragged into court."

"Have you ordered yet?" Affie asked, stretching like a cat before taking a seat on the stone bench. "I spent the last six hours dancing at an embassy reception and I could use a pick-me-upper."

"Did Dietro come?"

"Work dancing, with visiting businessmen," the Vergallian girl explained. "The next time Aleeytis asks me to stand in for her at one of those things I'm going to hold out for a favor."

"Is your workload lightening up now that the Alts have Earth Two to keep them busy?" Dorothy asked. "We need you back at the office."

"I wish. Earth Two has doubled my workload. Not only am I in endless negotiations with Flower over picking up groups of Alt colonists from Vergallian waystations for transport, the growing community of Alts on Union Station looks to me to help them acclimate to Humans. In fact, that's one of the things I want to talk to you about."

A Frunge female with her hair vines wound in a beehive style slipped into the grove and put a bowl of snacks on the table. "Are you ready to order?"

"I'll take whatever you have that's strong, pink, and won't poison me," Affie said.

"A Sleepy Time Moonshine for me," Flazint said. "Dorothy?"

"Do you have orange juice?"

"If we don't have a bottle in the fridge, we can send out," the waitress said.

"Are you still bringing Richard into the office every day?" Affie asked after the waitress departed. "I thought he'd be staying home more when he started eating solid food."

"Kevin is on and off the station today, and we're still adjusting to my dad not being there as a backup sitter."

"And you've never considered a daycare? Richard could socialize with other children and interact with adults of other species."

"He gets plenty of alien time at the office with Baa, Myst, Dietro, and—what are you hinting at?"

"Did you know that your brother runs a program on Flower to help the Alts acclimate to Humans before they arrive at Earth Two? I received a report from our representative on board that detailed all the best practices. The Alts do especially well when their initial encounters with Humans are with retired volunteers or toddlers. Alts quickly get over their fear of humanity when they're given the responsibility of caring for your children."

"Like when Methan's daughter Meena worked for InstaSitter and came to take care of Richard when I was doing sales seminars for franchisees?" Dorothy asked. "Working for InstaSitter could get anybody over their fears about other species in a hurry."

"I had a chance to prepare Meena before her first babysitting assignment, so she was a special case," Affie said. "But it planted the seed for an idea that the report from Flower has confirmed. I want to encourage the Alts to set up a daycare here on Union Station that their children can share with Human preschoolers as a way to get accustomed to you."

"And you want Richard for the beta tester? He started speaking early, but they call this age the Terrible Twos for a reason."

"I think it will be a big help if there's already a Human toddler present when parents come to inspect the facility, and it may be easier to convince the local Alts to participate when I can personally vouch for the first child."

"The office nursery is getting kind of small now that he'd rather be out of his playpen and toddling," Dorothy said. "When did you have in mind to talk to the Alts?"

"I thought if you'd loan him to me tomorrow, I'd bring him to the Vergallian embassy. Some Alts who are seeking advice about starting a daycare are coming to meet me, and I'll tell them that I'm watching Richard for you. Then I'll pretend an emergency came up and I have to run out for fifteen minutes. Knowing who they are, I'm sure they'll volunteer to help. From there it's just a matter of renting a space and finding more clients."

"That's so devious it will probably work," Flazint said with a laugh as the drinks arrived. "Did your royal training cover this sort of thing?"

"Royal training covers everything," Affie said with a barely suppressed grimace. She took a sip from the bubbly pink drink and sighed. "That hits the spot."

"Thank you," Dorothy said, relieved to find that the Frunge bartender hadn't added ice cubes to her orange juice. "How much do we owe you?"

"We're running a tab," Flazint said. "Don't tell me you're in a hurry to leave."

"It's evening for both of you, or maybe night for Affie," Dorothy said with a sigh. "I have a meeting with a fabric factory rep in forty minutes, and then the rest of my morning is booked with sales calls I'm covering for Dietro while he makes the final push on his *Mage Search* show. I don't remember the last time I got to spend a day just thinking about new design ideas."

"Maybe I can free up some time to help you when I come back to the office tomorrow," Flazint said. "You know I don't want to get involved with management at this point in my life, but I wouldn't mind helping vet new suppliers."

"You're just thinking of all the free samples you'll get," Affie said with a grin. "I miss working with you guys, but my hands are increasingly tied. The more I do to keep my family off my back, the higher my value goes on the marriage market for royals. They've been playing this game for millions of years and there's no way to win against them."

"I thought your family was willing to consider Dietro as long as he keeps his nose to the grindstone," Dorothy said.

"It would help if the new show is a success because the Grenouthians are giving him points in the production. But he's having trouble finding contestants with entertaining magical abilities."

"If I thought I could do magic, the last thing I would do is tell anybody," Flazint said. "Can you imagine what a matchmaker would say?"

"Plenty of Vergallian royals have gifts, but they aren't going to appear on a reality show," Affie said. "Dietro spends his free time chasing down rumors about illegitimate children who display special talents."

"Ping from Jyndal," Libby announced over Dorothy's implant.

"I'll take it," the EarthCent ambassador's daughter subvoced, and pointed at her ear to let her friends know.

"I'm sorry to ping you so early, but there's a journalist here from *Fashion Tomorrow* who says you told her to stop by any time for an interview."

"During regular office hours, not whenever she feels like it," Dorothy said in exasperation, and then reversed herself before the naïve young woman could repeat the message. "Tell her I'm on my way and I'll be there in less than five minutes." She dropped her hand and groaned. "There's a journalist from a Drazen fashion zine waiting at the office to see me. I have to go."

"I'm going to try to shift to Human Standard Time, so I'll see you tomorrow morning," Flazint said.

"And I'll stop by the office early to pick up Richard if that's acceptable to you," Affie added.

"I should check with Kevin, but I think he'll be okay with Richard playing beta tester for an Alt daycare experiment," Dorothy said. "Libby will be watching in any case." She worked the stroller out from behind the table and added, "Welcome back to Union Station, Flazint, and don't drink too much. See you guys tomorrow."

When Dorothy entered the offices of SBJ Fashions, Richard began a fair imitation of an emergency vehicle siren on Earth despite never having heard one. His mother shot the co-op student an apologetic look and hurried the two-year-old into the soundproof nursery. As soon as he knew that nobody would be able to hear his ear-piercing screams, Richard immediately settled down and began playing with blocks.

"Will you be all right while Mommy goes and talks to the nice Drazen lady, or do I need to get somebody to sit with you?" Dorothy asked.

"I building blocks," Richard replied as if he found the question silly.

"All right then. Just tell Libby if you need anything." Dorothy glanced up at the ceiling, mouthed, "Thank you," and then hurried out to meet the journalist.

"Hinka," the Drazen introduced herself. "*Fashion Tomorrow.*"

"Dorothy Crick. I've met hundreds of Drazen females but you're the first Hinka."

"It means I'm a divorced mother. No, don't apologize," Hinka continued before Dorothy could overcome her surprise. "Divorce is rare, but it does happen, and it saved me from murder."

"Your husband was trying to kill you?" Dorothy asked before she could stop herself.

"My apologies. I took an accelerated course in Humanese and I don't speak it very well. I should have said it saved me from murdering."

"You mean becoming a murderer. That's very—surprising."

"So was my husband," Hinka said. "Is there somewhere we can sit and talk without the risk of being turned into something?"

"What do you—oh. Jyndal isn't that advanced, and Baa would never do anything that could impact her equity stake. She's a part owner in SBJ Fashions."

"A seat would still be nice. I'm not fond of work stools."

"Of course," Dorothy said, thinking that the journalist was the most plain-spoken Drazen female she'd ever met. "We can use the breakroom. But I wasn't expecting you this morning and I have a rep from a Frunge factory due in about twenty-five minutes."

"This won't take that long. I just have a few questions about—drumroll."

"Drumroll?"

"The future," the Drazen said, her throaty English sounding a bit disappointed. "I thought that 'drumroll' was a Human idiom inviting listeners to guess what's coming next."

"I just didn't expect it in this context," Dorothy said as she led the Drazen into the conference room. "Did you learn our language just to interview me?"

Hinka burst out laughing and ended up having to cover her mouth with her tentacle for the sake of manners. "I suppose I'll have to get used to that question," she said when she recovered. "*Fashion Tomorrow* is initiating coverage of humanity, and my editor thought it would sell a few extra subscriptions to start with the daughter of EarthCent's president."

"Acting president, it's only for six months."

"My editor will make that decision," Hinka said. "I've read up about you in the Galactic Free Press, so I won't waste time asking questions about your past. What's in the future for Dorothy Crick and SBJ Fashions?"

"Like, tomorrow, or the future-future?"

"Ah, I understand your confusion. *Fashion Tomorrow* isn't a literal description of our coverage. It's the closest Humanese translation for a line from a famous poem by Worc in which he refers to the ephemeral nature of blooming flowers and wonders what their fashion will be tomorrow."

"That's a pretty depressing word-picture," Dorothy said as she went over to the coffee station. "Would you like a cup?"

"Do you have Instant Inca?" Hinka asked.

"You're in luck. My mom knows the principal stakeholder of Drazen Foods and he sent her a case that I stole for the office. But don't use that in your story."

"My editor makes all of those decisions," the journalist said noncommittally. "You did agree to be recorded when we talked earlier. It's the only way I work."

"I suppose," Dorothy said, hoping that *Fashion Today* was read by Drazens who shopped for clothes, and not some highbrow publication with a misleading name. "I guess the answer to your question is that we plan to keep growing and see where our nanofabric franchises take us."

"You mean, if you saw your sales shifting to a new species or demographic, you'd target your future design activity to match."

"We're very data-driven, though if our sales shifted that way, it would probably mean we were already succeeding with the growing market segment. Since SBJ Fashions was founded with the goal of cross-species fashion design, we try not to over-commit to any single vertical."

"Are you still working on a cross-species Golden Ratio?"

"I thought we weren't going to talk about the past."

"Just asking," the Drazen said with a smile as Dorothy handed over a mug of Instant Inca. "A little bird told me that you've been selected for a second season to provide an epic jewelry set for the LARPing tournament."

"The regular season league play," Dorothy corrected the journalist, and then wondered if she had just given away information. "Most of my time these days goes into adopting designs for easy stitching on treadle sewing machines so they can qualify as second-tier handmade, plus a lot of business planning."

"You've replaced Shaina Cohan? According to my notes, she was the business brains of the outfit."

"I haven't replaced her. It's just that she doesn't exactly come into the office anymore, at least not very often. She and her sister Brinda are taking care of the *All Species Cookbook* while my mom and her special assistant are away on Earth. And Dietro does all the sales projections, but he prefers for me to handle the production scheduling since I have a better feel for how long it will take to change between designs and fabrics."

"Doesn't every fashion house use multiple fabric manufacturers to avoid supply-chain bottlenecks?"

"It's more than alternative vendors with us," Dorothy said, waxing enthusiastic as the Instant Inca kicked in its caffeine boost. "Even though some of our dresses look almost identical when they're worn by models, humanoids from various species have different proportions, sometimes subtle, sometimes obvious, like the extra set of arms on Dollnicks. But there are even bigger differences in how the fabrics feel against our skin, and some species prohibit certain mixtures of fibers. I can show you my spreadsheet—"

"Maybe another time," Hinka interrupted. "I have to admit that my research didn't show this side of your personality. Did you take business courses at the Open University?"

"Just the required ones, and I didn't pay much attention. I wasn't that interested in business until Jeeves threw me into the pool to make me swim. Myst's fiancé, Lancelot, is a computer whiz, and he got me started on spreadsheets. Now I'm kind of addicted to working the numbers rather than just settling for whatever Jeeves will approve."

"And what is it like working directly for a Stryx?" the Drazen asked. "Does he ever express an opinion about fashion?"

"Jeeves has opinions about everything, but SBJ Fashions is strictly business for him. The only time I've ever seen a Stryx wear clothes was when Metoo came to my wedding in a tux."

"The infamous SBJ Fashions commercial," Hinka said with a smile. "Save the gown! I almost ran out and bought one myself. My ex-husband would have thrown a fit if I'd asked him to turn our wedding into an advertisement."

Dorothy took a sip from her coffee rather than admitting that Jeeves had sprung the commercial on them as a surprise to recoup the wedding expenses he'd offered to cover. "If you're interested in the marketing side of the business you should interview Dietro," she said. "I come up with ideas sometimes, but he's the one who handles all of our outside sales and relations with boutiques."

"The Vergallian. I think they're going into evening hours now if I remember my clock alignments, unless he works on Human Standard Time."

"Sometimes, but he also works a lot more hours than I do," Dorothy said. "Except I forgot he's not coming in this week and I'm handling some of his sales calls later."

"That's fine, he doesn't tie in with the president-of-EarthCent angle. Do you dress your mother?"

"Do I—no, but she buys dresses from us, especially the cross-species version of the Frunge business suits with skirt wraps."

"I've seen pictures, she looks like a conservative dresser. Is SBJ Fashions showing at the New World's Fair?"

"We have booth space in the Human Empire pavilion because so much of our production has moved to Flower and she's hosting their headquarters."

"Your brother being the emperor wouldn't have anything to do with it?" the Drazen asked with a sly smile.

"Samuel has nothing to do with SBJ Fashions," Dorothy said. "He modeled in a few fashion shows for us years ago, but I doubt he can tell a ball gown from a tube dress."

"Despite being an accomplished ballroom dancer?"

"All right, maybe that was a bad example. We never talk about the business, and I don't think he wears anything we make."

"The emperor has no clothes."

"What? I didn't say that."

"It makes a catchy headline, don't you think?"

Nine

"But why?" Grace asked her father plaintively. "It's the weekend, and you have to come to my recital tomorrow."

"The other Union Station ambassadors live according to different clocks and calendars," Daniel explained. "The chairman of the Galactic Historical Sites Commission is a Verlock, and he scheduled the meeting for first thing in his morning."

"Uncle Srythlan? I'll ask him to change it."

"Mike and I will be at the recital," Shaina told Grace. "I'll save it on my implant and show it to your father later."

"I can't go," Mike said. "I have to do a training thing for camp."

"Didn't you have a full week's training last year?"

"It's a refresher."

"Come on, Princess," Daniel said, setting aside his coffee and getting up from the couch. "I'll read you a bedtime story."

"You have to get going or you won't be early," Shaina told him. "I'll read the story, Grace. And Mike, you have to take Queenie for her late walk because your father might not be back until morning."

"Can I go by Mac's Bones so Queenie can visit with Alexander?" Mike asked.

Daniel and Shaina exchanged a look while the Cayl hound broke off her evening stretching routine and began paying attention.

"Ping Fenna first and tell her to ask her parents," his mother said. "Nine in the evening is pretty late to show up unannounced."

Mike mumbled something, still unaccustomed to subvocalizing for his new implant, and everybody waited silently while Fenna received parental approval for the visit. Then he gave Queenie the nod, and the two of them bolted for the door.

"No later than eleven," Daniel called after the fifteen-year-old. "Keep him out of trouble, Queenie."

"Eleven?" Shaina asked her husband after Mike left.

"It's the weekend, and he's almost sixteen," the associate ambassador said. "If the meeting only goes for a few hours, I'll be able to come to your recital, Princess."

"You were gone a whole day for the last Historical meeting," Grace said with a pout.

"That was the first one, and Srythlan read the minutes from the final meeting of the commission on Corner Station. I wasn't the only ambassador to fall asleep."

"Don't be surprised if you see Bob Steelforth there," Shaina told her husband as he began to get ready. "When I was working on the cookbook with Judith at the embassy today, she mentioned that he'd be covering both of the new commissions on Union Station."

"That's great," Daniel said, taking his satchel off the hook on the rack where the family hung their assorted school bags and such. "Having a reporter present may speed things up."

"Don't the other species cover the commission meetings? I thought they were all public."

"They are, which I suspect is the reason Srythlan took a full day reading those minutes. If that doesn't stop the public from showing up, I don't know what will."

Daniel went by the Little Apple along the way to buy a large take-out coffee, and when he exited the lift tube on the Verlock deck, he found the Galactic Free Press reporter waiting outside of the embassy.

"Associate Ambassador Cohan," Bob greeted Daniel. "I'm surprised Ofer didn't come with you as he has such an interest in history."

"He's out with his girlfriend. Is something up?"

"I got here early to do a quick interview with Ambassador Srythlan, and he said they're going to move the meeting to the embassy conference room due to lack of public interest. I wanted to check if you'd be okay with my sitting behind you."

"As long as you're wearing your press badge, I don't think anybody will confuse you with an advisor," Daniel said. "I'm not sure what to expect after the circus Srythlan put on last week."

"I'm sorry I missed it," Bob said without a trace of sarcasm. "I watched the summary on the Grenouthian news, and the announcer kept cutting away to a fictional breaking story about paint drying. It was pretty amusing."

"As long as they didn't show me sleeping with my mouth open. When Ambassador Crute woke me up for one of the snack breaks, I realized I'd been drooling."

"Ambassador Srythlan told me that you'll be voting on the schedule and agenda for the next ten meetings tonight, so at least there will be some excitement. And I brought a thermos just in case," he added, patting his shoulder bag.

"I'm going to start drinking mine as soon as we sit down, so if the meeting only goes a few hours, I'll be able to get to sleep afterward. Don't you worry that nursing it will just keep you up all night regardless?"

"The baby is still waking up at night, so it doesn't matter." Then Bob's face assumed an earnest look that Daniel associated with the reporter going on the record. "I've been doing some research into the commission's scope of responsibility, and I got hung up on the difference between Galactic Historical Sites and Galactic Heritage Sites," he said as the two men entered the Verlock embassy. "Any insight?"

"We have a sovereign human community on a Heritage site, over two million people working there, and Flower has stopped a couple of times. Other than the archaeological workers and their support, it's a dead world with no development, and I gather the Stryx intend to keep it that way."

"So you're saying that Heritage Sites are associated with extinct species."

"I think that's how it works," Daniel said as they passed the lava feature in the lobby where a flow of molten rock cascaded through artificial falls into a pool that was pumped back up to the top. "To the best of my knowledge, the Heritage sites exist outside the framework of the tunnel network treaty, and they're located throughout the galaxy. It's the only instance I'm aware of where the Stryx don't acknowledge the sovereignty of the empires or entities that claim the local space. When they designate a world as a Galactic Heritage Site and leave warning satellites or beacons, anybody who tries to take anything from the surface without permission is doing so at their own risk."

"And the only sentients I'm aware of who gamble on the Stryx not noticing are the Wanderers, and even they have the sense to keep their pilfering to a few souvenirs," the

Horten ambassador joined the conversation at the door to the conference room.

"Ambassador Ortha," Daniel greeted him. "I'm sorry I haven't gotten back to you yet about the—" he hesitated for a moment when he saw the Horten's eyes flick to the reporter, "—thing, but I passed it on to Flower."

"Thank you," the Horten said, leading the way into the room. "There's no hurry."

"Journalist Steelforth," the Grenouthian ambassador addressed Bob formally, as the reporter took a chair against the wall behind Daniel's seat at the enormous rock slab that served as a conference table. "If you're here to report on the commission moving to Union Station, I'm afraid you've been scooped."

"I'm here for background," Bob explained. "Even if nothing happens in the next few meetings, I hope to learn something about how commissions operate."

"You should come to my Gambling Commission," the Thark ambassador joined in from the other side of the table. "We deal with issues of immediate concern."

"I'm planning to attend the next meeting. From a reporter's standpoint, covering diplomacy on a Stryx station can be frustrating because most of the committee meetings where policy is decided are closed."

"And why do you think commission meetings are always open to the public?" the Horten ambassador asked.

Bob thought for a moment before replying. "Because they deal with issues the Stryx want publicized for some reason?"

Ortha reached for a slice of some alien fruit arranged on a jade platter before replying. "Does the Horten idiom 'Trial Balloon' translate properly for you?"

"We have that one too," the Fillinduck ambassador commented as he slipped through the space between where Bob was sitting against the wall and the occupied chairs at the table. "I hadn't realized that balloons were freighted with universal meaning."

"What are we discussing?" Bork asked, taking the seat next to Daniel. "The history of balloons? I attended a festival on one of our worlds for aviation reenactors and there was a balloon regatta that stretched over the horizon."

"Idioms," Ortha said. "In the context of why commission meetings are public and committee meetings are private. I suggested that open meetings serve as trial balloons."

The Drazen ambassador made a show of looking around the conference room, nodding to Czeros and Crute as the Frunge and Dollnick ambassadors entered together. "Only if the public attends."

"Ambassador Gem," Daniel greeted the clone as she took the seat on his other side. He produced a large bar of Swiss chocolate from his satchel and passed it to her. "Kelly sent this for you in the diplomatic bag and said that there's more where that came from. It sounds like a high proportion of the pavilions at the New World's Fair feature foodstuffs."

"I'll have to remember to bring a large suitcase and pack light when I go so I'll have room for goodies," Gwendolyn said.

Srythlan, who had been conspicuously absent to this point, shuffled slowly in, accompanied by the Vergallian ambassador, Aleeytis, and Affie, the Alt's contract queen on Union station. Then the Chert ambassador deactivated his shoulder-mounted invisibility projector and materialized in his chair. Everybody did a silent head count to see if any of their diplomatic colleagues were missing, and then the Verlock ambassador began to speak at his best pace.

"I declare this meeting of the Galactic Historical Sites Commission to be in session. I would like to extend a special welcome to Affie, who is attending unofficially as the Alt representative. There's no need to read the minutes from the last meeting as they consisted wholly of previous minutes, so if there are no questions, we'll proceed with electing officers. Yes, Ambassador Crute?"

"Why is it necessary to announce that Contract Queen Affie is attending unofficially when this meeting is already open to the public?" the Dollnick asked. "Is there some legal purpose to your statement?"

Srythlan nodded ponderously. "The issue of the Alt homeworld is on tonight's agenda, so I thought it appropriate to extend to her a special invitation and officially acknowledge her unofficial presence for the record. Yes, Ortha?"

"Which Alt homeworld?"

"I'd prefer to leave that until after the election. Does anybody wish to stand for secretary?"

There was a long pause as all the ambassadors tried to avoid each other's gaze, and Srythlan let out a rumbling sigh. "Very well," he said and reached under the table to produce a device that looked like a wall clock with one hand. He placed it face up on the table and gave it a good shove like he was playing shuffleboard without a cue. It stopped exactly halfway down the stone slab. "Would you do the honors, Bork?"

The Drazen extended his tentacle and imparted a strong spin to the hand of what Daniel now recognized was a selection device with sections proportioned to give equal probability to the arrow pointing at any one of the seated ambassadors. The room went completely still as the rotation began to slow, and then Aleeytis let out a groan when the arrow stopped in the division that mapped to the location of her chair.

"Best out of three?" she suggested.

"Secretary Aleeytis will henceforth be responsible for reading the minutes recorded and transcribed by the Union Station librarian," Srythlan announced ponderously. "Will anybody volunteer for vice-chair, or shall I ask Ambassador Bork to give the selector another spin."

"What's involved?" Daniel asked, and immediately regretted the question as a dozen heads swiveled in his direction.

"He's never served as a commission officer," the Grenouthian ambassador observed. "Doesn't that mean he should be appointed by default?"

"Is that a motion?" Srythlan asked.

"I move that Associate Ambassador Cohan be appointed vice-chair on the grounds that he's never served as an officer on a commission."

"All in favor?"

Ambassador Gem shot Daniel a guilty look and waited for him to nod before raising her hand. It wouldn't have made a difference in the outcome as all the other ambassadors had at least one hand up.

"Vice Chair Cohan. Do you wish to make an acceptance speech for the record?"

"I just want to know what the job involves," Daniel said.

"It's merely a formality," Srythlan said, eliciting a few chuckles from around the table. "As we're all required to be present at every meeting, you won't be called upon to stand in for me unless some untoward event should keep me away, which is highly unlikely. Your only main duty is to serve as spokesperson for the commission should we garner enough attention to make that necessary. Now, does anybody object to this morning's agenda?"

"Evening's agenda," Daniel muttered under his breath.

"Why do we have to review the status of the abandoned Brupt worlds?" Czeros asked. "The Stryx kicked them out of the galaxy millions of years ago and the planets have been languishing on the market ever since."

"Because they're booby-trapped," the Grenouthian ambassador observed.

"Booby-trapped or not, if the Stryx put them up for sale, doesn't that imply that they're of no historical importance?"

"You were here last week," Srythlan said. "The agenda was set by the last incarnation of the commission and the reasons were given in the minutes. Do you want me to read—"

"No!" all of the ambassadors shouted at the same time, drawing a slow smile from the chair.

"Very well, then. In deference to Contract Queen Affie, whose interest in our proceedings is no doubt limited to our consideration of the status of the Alt homeworld, we'll begin with Earth."

"Earth?" Daniel asked. "My Earth?"

"I object to the characterization of the third planet in the Sol system as his Earth," Affie said immediately.

"This isn't a court of law, and you're officially here unofficially," Srythlan reminded her. "Associate Ambassador Cohan, please refrain from making statements our guest may find inflammatory to Alt sensibilities."

"But the Alts abandoned Earth over thirty thousand years ago," Daniel protested.

"I object to the characterization of the Alts departure from the third planet of the Sol system as abandonment," Affie said. "They were being hounded to extinction by aggressive Humans, bringing about a Stryx intervention."

"I withdraw my unfortunate choice of words. I meant to say that the Alts have since built a glorious new history on a planet of their own, and I would think that's the world they would wish to see designated a historical site."

"The nomination of the third planet in the Sol system as a Galactic Historical Site didn't come from myself or any other contract queens working for the Alts."

Daniel looked from Srythlan to Affie to Aleeytis. "Then I'm confused."

"Without returning to the minutes to which you all so strenuously objected, I can summarize that the request for this commission to consider the historical status of Earth came from an automated system created by the Stryx," the Verlock ambassador said.

"Do you mean that every homeworld of a new species is automatically considered a historical site?"

"Considered *for* a historical site designation," Srythlan said, putting his stress on the preposition."

"And how come you don't object when he calls it Earth?" Daniel asked Affie.

"Ambassador Srythlan isn't speaking English and you're getting a Human-context translation on your implant," the Vergallian told him.

"Sorry," Daniel said, embarrassed to have made such a rookie blunder.

"I saw nothing in the minutes suggesting that the Galactic Historical Site review is based on the emergence of

Humans or Alts from Earth," Srythlan continued. "The point is, it's at the top of our agenda, and I think it makes sense to do the site visit while our colleague Ambassador McAllister is in a position to cut through any red tape for us on the ground."

"Are you making a motion?" the Grenouthian ambassador asked facetiously.

"I motion that the members of this commission schedule a site visit to Earth before Ambassador McAllister completes her term as EarthCent's acting president."

"Second the motion," Bork said immediately.

"Third," Czeros and Ortha said at the same time.

"Any objection?" the Verlock ambassador asked.

"Is this all a ploy so you can visit the New World's Fair without taking vacation time?" Daniel asked.

"Are you stating an objection?"

"Just asking."

"Then the motion is passed unanimously. Vice Chair Cohan will of course be responsible for coordinating travel arrangements with the Stryx, which will be paid for out of the commission's fund for site visits. Yes, Daniel?"

"As you all know, I'm new to sitting on commissions and have never made a site visit, historical or otherwise. Could somebody fill me in on the basics, so I know what we're discussing?"

"It's a literal translation," Ortha told Daniel, in case the associate ambassador was worried that 'site visit' was an idiom expressing something unrelated to the two words.

"It's all expenses paid," Bork told him. "What else do you need to know?"

"But it's not all fun and games," the Chert ambassador spoke up uncharacteristically. "There will be a list of historically significant sites at the destination that we're required to visit as a group."

"May I suggest the cave art created by the Alts on the Iberian Peninsula before Humans arrived on the scene?" Affie asked.

"Cave art," Srythlan said, nodding his head. "An excellent choice. Daniel? Do you have any preferred destinations?"

"I'm not much of a historian so I'd rather consult with my colleagues if we don't have to get this all done right now," Daniel said. "You told us that the site inspection is due to an automatic scheduling mechanism. Did that come with any pre-selected destinations?"

"Yes, but when I transferred the coordinates to a map, two of the locations were underwater and the third is covered by an ice cap, so you'll have to plan accordingly."

"I need to reserve a submarine?"

"Practically all spacecraft capable of landing in a planet's gravitational field are submersible," the Dollnick ambassador told him. "The trick is choosing one with sufficient portholes that we won't all be viewing the site via remote cameras."

"Isn't the pressure under the ocean much greater than the pressure in space?" Daniel asked.

"Space is a vacuum, the absence of pressure, but an excellent question nonetheless," Srythlan said. "While I'm sure a few species somewhere must still build submersibles with high-pressure portholes for deep descents, any spaceship will be equipped with an atmosphere retention field that can be tuned to repel water, though the power drain will be proportional to the pressure."

"When you said I'd be coordinating travel arrangements with the Stryx, I assumed you were talking about dealing with a tour agency."

"We need complete autonomy and the ability to go anywhere on Earth, including entering the craters of active volcanoes. If you're going to work through a travel agency, I would suggest finding one that has extensive experience dealing with non-Human tourists from the tunnel network."

"Do you think that descending into the crater of an active volcano will be necessary?" Daniel asked after making a few notes on his tab.

"Chairman's prerogative," the Verlock said. "I'm not going to go all the way to Earth and miss out on the sights worth seeing. I hear there are quite a few active volcanoes under the sea."

Ten

"Just stay close, Joe, and if you feel even the slightest bit funny, tell me," Kelly said through the fixed smile she had pasted on the moment that the floating limousines carrying the delegation from the Empire of a Hundred Worlds appeared.

"It's nice to know that you still see me that way, Kelly, but the expiration date on worrying about upper caste Vergallians using their pheromones to temporarily enslave me as a boy-toy passed at least three decades ago."

"I've never seen such a graceful security detail," Colonel Davidson observed as a group of Vergallians flowed out of the limousines and created a cordon. "They move like dancers."

"I'm sure they all are," Kelly said, trying to draw herself up a little straighter, though the effort turned her smile into something more like a grimace.

"Just relax, Kel," Joe said. "You've met queens before, and this time, you're a president rather than an ambassador. Aabina will make sure everything goes smoothly."

"I don't like the way that queen has her hand on Aabina's arm. It's like she's trying to stake a claim."

The colonel shielded her mouth with a hand and muttered, "I just saw the one in the white suit staring at you and then saying something to the queen. I think she's a lip reader."

"Oh, fudge," Kelly said.

After that, they remained silent until the Vergallian delegation arrived at the gate and Aabina made the introductions.

"I've been instructed to offer the full cooperation of the New York Guard," Colonel Davidson said after names, ranks, and titles were exchanged. "I can assign a liaison officer or accompany you myself if you prefer."

"I'm sure my bodyguards are capable of handling any situation that might come up," Queen Asiedu replied in English. "My truthsayer—" she inclined her head slightly towards her companion, who was dressed all in white, "—will ensure that our party doesn't draw any undue attention from the crowd."

"Queen Asiedu wants to start with the Human Empire pavilion to make sure she's not pressed for time," Aabina told Kelly, a clear cue that they had been standing at the gate long enough. "Her schedule only allows her one day on Earth."

"I understand," Kelly said, trying to hide her relief that she wouldn't be stuck hosting the current head of the Council of Queens for a week. "It's about a twenty-minute walk to the Human Empire pavilion from here, Queen Asiedu. If you'd prefer transportation, I can arrange for—"

"That won't be necessary," the most powerful Vergallian in the Empire of a Hundred Worlds told her. "A short walk will give us a chance to get better acquainted."

Despite her initial misgivings, Kelly found Queen Asiedu to be an attentive conversationalist who expressed an interest in most of the cultural exhibits they passed. Thanks to all the stops, the twenty-minute walk had already gone over an hour when they encountered a particularly dense section of the crowd, and the queen's

Vergallian security detail declined to push through for operational reasons.

"It looks like everybody is gathered for some sort of public debate," Joe told Kelly, who wasn't wearing heels and couldn't see anything over the bodyguards immediately in front of her.

"Who holds debates at a fair?"

"The banner says it's the Ladies in Waiting. And two women just climbed onto the stage."

"The Ladies in Waiting?" Queen Asiedu asked. "They send a petition to the Council of Queens at least once a cycle. For fans of royal government, they appear to be woefully uninformed on matters of protocol. I meant to ask if the movement is officially sanctioned by EarthCent."

"I've heard of them, but that's all," Kelly said. "They don't have a presence on Union Station, and I only arrived on Earth recently. Do you know anything about them, Aabina?"

"The Ladies in Waiting started as a fan group for Vergallian dramas but it's since turned into a movement to establish royal governments on Earth. I understand that there's a schism between the women who want to establish new royal lines by elevating members, and those who want to invite Vergallian princesses to serve as contract queens."

"Then it is the group that keeps sending the council petitions," Queen Asiedu said. "I would be interested in hearing what they have to say."

Aabina brought out her smartphone and had a brief conversation with someone. "Larry can meet us backstage in ten minutes and get us seats," she told them. "He checked our positions on the map and said that if we cut to the left behind the Antarctica pavilion, we can approach the Ladies in Waiting stage from the one direction it's unobstructed."

The queen's bodyguards passed around Aabina's phone to study the map, approved of the plan, and the delegation worked its way through the thinning crowd into the noticeably chilly air surrounding the pavilion that featured penguins taking turns on an ice slide and fishing in an artificial saltwater pool.

Whatever the truthsayer was doing to make the delegation and its inhumanly beautiful upper caste Vergallians unnoticeable to the surrounding crowds also prevented anybody from questioning what the group was doing in an area reserved for employees and volunteers. When they arrived at the back of the stage, Larry was waiting and escorted them all into the wings, where half a dozen folding chairs had been set out. Kelly thankfully took a seat between Joe and Queen Asiedu just as the younger of the two women on stage wrapped up her opening statement.

"You know how back on Union Station when you tell an alien that you're from Earth, they always ask as a joke if you're related to so-and-so?" Joe whispered in Kelly's ear. "Larry said that the older woman who's about to speak is his mother-in-law."

"My name is Janice, and I'm the chapter head of the Ladies in Waiting for a county in the northern part of the city-state that's known primarily for headquarters and factory city of Drazen Foods located there," the speaker began. "As you can see, I'm a few years older than my opposite number in today's debate, and the fact that I've lived within sight of the elevator stalk since it was built and pretended it wasn't there should tell you something about my background."

There was a loud murmur mixed with derisive laughing from the crowd, and a few cries of "Alien denier," to which Janice merely nodded in agreement.

"Having seen, or to be brutally honest, been shown the error of my ways, I've dedicated my energy to becoming part of the solution. This led me to an examination of best practices in running societies and planets, and as the old saying goes, a trillion Vergallians can't be wrong."

This brought a rousing cheer from the crowd, and Kelly glanced to her left just in time to see a brilliant smile add to Queen Asiedu's already unearthly beauty.

"But there's a difference of opinion among the Ladies in Waiting between those of us who believe that Earth needs genuine Vergallian royals, bred and trained to the task of governing, and those like my youthful opponent, who wish to see a new human elite established. And I couldn't help noticing how she detailed her educational achievements, the unpaid internships at non-governmental organizations, even her ascent of Mount Everest on the back of a Sherpa—"

Janice was interrupted by gales of laughter and an angry protest from the younger woman before continuing.

"I exaggerate for the sake of illustration, but my point is that the highly accomplished young woman to my right sounds like she is running for the office of queen—"

This time the interruption included loud booing, and studying the tightly packed crowd, Kelly thought she spotted Georgia's face over the shoulder of a short woman wearing a Ladies in Waiting T-shirt.

"—and, and," Janice continued, pausing for a moment while the last cries died out, "and while I'm sure she's eminently qualified to run a charity, there's more to being a queen than going on listening tours and handing out other people's money."

"She seems quite intelligent," Queen Asiedu commented to Kelly.

"I have an admission to make," Janice said in a quiet voice that was such a changeup the audience unconsciously leaned forward as if that would help them hear. "I saw my first Vergallian drama two years ago, and it was like a light suddenly going on in my head and revealing all the hidden thoughts and desires that I spent five decades storing up without ever realizing they were there. I lived in a commune where we all agreed to work for the common good, but somehow it turned into an endless clash of egos, and the desire, above all, to prove ourselves more righteous than our neighbors. I was so blinded by my own certainty that I sacrificed my relationship with my daughter, and for what?"

"What?" Queen Asiedu asked, leaning forward in her seat.

"All for the sake of being the center of my own universe where I was always right and everything I did was always justified," Janice said, her voice now rising. "But episode forty-two of the six-hundred-and-thirteenth season of *Green Fields, Gold Crown,* drove away the shadows like a newborn star. Suddenly I knew, I knew in my bones, that we can all accomplish so much more working together under competent royal leadership than making every detail of life into a battle over who's in charge."

"Time," the younger woman cried. "She's already twelve seconds over."

"Twelve seconds," Janice scoffed. "If that's all you have to say we may as well stop now and vote."

"Vote! Vote!" the crowd began to chant, and when the younger woman tried to speak, she was drowned out, though Joe suspected that the microphone pickup she was wearing had been switched off. Then his smartphone vibrated in his pocket, and he took it out to find a push notification that read, "Download Ladies in Waiting Voting App (Y/N)?"

"I guess," he said out loud, tapping the 'Y'.

"What are you doing?" Kelly asked.

"Not sure yet," Joe said, displaying the phone. "Didn't you get a notification? I see Aabina has her phone out."

"I turned it off. There's no way I was going to take a call or check a text while I'm with the leader of the Empire of a Hundred Worlds."

The queen said something to her truthsayer, who passed the message to Aabina, but the latter shook her head and pointed back at Kelly and Joe. Then Queen Asiedu asked Kelly, "Can you see what they're voting on? Aabina couldn't install the program because she's registered as non-Human."

"It's done," Joe said and tapped the new icon. "Ladies in Waiting official voting app for attendees at the New World's Fair. There are only two options. I can choose to invite Vergallian princesses to Earth to rule as contract queens, or to establish a system to elect queens by the popular vote."

"That would be a disaster," Queen Asiedu said. "Sound rulers would never win a popularity contest."

"So what are you voting for?" Kelly asked.

"I don't live here, it wouldn't be fair," Joe said. "If you asked me to vote on whether or not we should invite a Vergallian princess to represent the human community on Union Station, that would be a different matter."

"Wise man," the queen said. "You make a fine consort for a president."

"Look," he said, showing the phone again. "It's tallying the votes in real time and adding them to the previous totals. I guess they've been doing these debates several times a week because there's already over a hundred thousand votes logged."

"Sixty-one percent in favor of inviting Vergallian princesses to come and rule Earth," Kelly said ruefully as she looked at the screen. "I'm not sure whether that's good or bad."

"It demonstrates remarkable intelligence on the part of the fairgoers, but I don't know how representative they are of this planet's inhabitants on the whole," Queen Asiedu said thoughtfully. "Perhaps I'll have to take another look at those petitions when I return home."

The phone vibrated again, and Joe saw an incoming text from the Human Empire's Minister of Trade. "It's Larry," he announced. "His wife told him that the debate ended early, and he wants to know when we're coming so he can meet us."

They exited the stage the way they had entered and made their way to the giant circus tent that housed the Human Empire pavilion. Larry met them at the front entrance and escorted them inside.

"Was that woman, Janice, really your mother-in-law?" Kelly asked. "She's a very effective speaker."

"Hidden depths," Larry said. "Don't mention it around Georgia, though. Bit of a mother-daughter rivalry thing there."

"I'd like to meet her later if she has time," Queen Asiedu said unexpectedly. "Do you think she'll be willing?"

"I think she'll be tongue-tied, at least for thirty seconds or so, but I can't imagine she'll pass up the opportunity. Are you staying in town?"

"My royal yacht is in the short-term parking area." She turned to her truthsayer and asked, "Second-to-last stop on the monorail?"

"I believe so, Highness," her companion murmured.

"It's fortunate I took the time to learn Humanese before visiting," Queen Asiedu continued. "I don't suppose an alien-denier living on a commune would have received a translation implant."

"The commune also had a tech-ban of sorts," Larry said. "It's why she never had a smartphone until recently. My wife tells horror stories about growing up without one."

"I understand that they're one of the three technologies that received protection when the Stryx opened Earth, but I had in mind something much bulkier, like a teacher bot. It would be interesting to learn more about them."

"Then you're in luck because smartphones are one of the highlights of our exhibits. Between the hardware, the operating system software, and the apps, they've spawned an entire ecosystem that stretches from Earth to Flower. Ironically, smartphones were once seen as a steppingstone to virtual reality technology that never quite lived up to its promise, but it's recently been revived as a sort of cut-rate Stryxnet conferencing solution that lowers bandwidth expenses by more than ninety percent. We used it extensively in the run-up to the fair, and..." The Human Empire's minister of trade trailed off when he realized he was walking with Joe and that the women and bodyguards had all fallen behind. "What happened?"

"SBJ Fashions," Joe said. "I'm not sure the queen has ever seen a nanofabric demonstration before and we walked right by one in progress."

The two men backtracked to where the Vergallian delegation was watching a Drazen tourist who had volunteered for a public fashion makeover, putting the nanofabric technology to the test. The young boutique assistant, who was operating the programming device that instructed the nanobots what pattern to assume next, whispered something to the volunteer, and then tapped an override button on the screen and touched it to the fringe of the skirt of the ball gown.

Except for the queen's bodyguards who were facing away from the demonstration, everyone stared as the gown morphed into a tube dress while a stream of nanobots broke off from the main and flowed down the Drazen's tentacle, causing her to giggle, before forming a matching sleeve. The audience broke into gasps of disbelief and applause, and then the bodyguards had all they could handle to prevent the queen from getting caught in the crush as women surged forward demanding to sign up for their own fashion makeover.

"The fittings are very popular," Larry told the queen when she reluctantly turned her back on the booth. The Drazen female slipped into the changing room, after placing her order for three of the outfits she'd tried on by means of the nanofabric. "We tripled the size of their booth just before the opening and it's worked out very well for them."

"I seem to recall that your daughter is a part owner in the business," Queen Asiedu said to Kelly.

"Dorothy is the lead designer, but if she's been given an ownership stake, I must have forgotten about it," Earth-

Cent's acting president replied. "The nanofabric is a Gem invention."

The queen didn't exactly flinch, but Kelly picked up on the slight chill and changed the subject. "My daughter has also become an avid fan of treadle-powered sewing machines, and she brought one home from Flower that had been purchased on a Vergallian tech-ban world."

"Sewing was the first useful skill I acquired in life, unless you count mucking out the royal stables," Queen Asiedu said with a half-smile. "Both activities were a welcome break from the more cerebral components of royal training." She glanced up and her eyes widened in surprise, though not as much as when the nanofabric had reflowed to create a silky sleeve on the Drazen's tentacle. "Multi-story tents?"

"It's from a human factory on a Frunge open world," Larry explained. "The technology is licensed, but the designs are inspired by the circus tents that were common on our world for centuries before the Stryx brought us onto the tunnel network. The smartphone technology exhibit is located in the next section, but I'd be happy to take you through the upper stories where smaller manufacturers from sovereign human communities are displaying."

The truthsayer brought her lips near the queen's ear as they walked, and murmured something which drew a smile in response. "My briefing referenced a product that was paired in some way with your smartphones and offers a method for Humans to locate family members through genetic tracing."

"GenePost," Larry affirmed. "The booth is right next to the smartphone exhibit since they distribute an app for phones or tablets."

"If you tell me that you can sequence a genome using one of those smartphones, I'll buy one myself to have it reverse-engineered in the imperial labs," Queen Asiedu said. "Can they have advanced that far, Aabina?"

"The genetic test is done separately by mailing in a postcard with a blood sample," Aabina explained.

"Regular mail?"

"The capture technology employs 3D printed carbon nanotubes," Larry added. "It was developed by a Farling who lives on board Flower."

Queen Asiedu came to a momentary halt and glanced over at her truthsayer, who gave an almost imperceptible nod. "Will wonders never cease," the queen said under her breath in Vergallian, and then she saw the giant inflatable smartphone balloon organic LED screen suspended over the exhibit and broke out laughing. "That's more of what I had in mind for the size of a genetic sequencing device engineered by Humans. But what is the young woman on the screen supposed to be doing?"

"It's a scene from the game *A Mazing Earth*, which was developed by humans on Bits before they mainly moved to Flower. The mobile version has become quite popular on Earth, even though it was targeted for the cross-species market."

The queen's bodyguards, moving with their usual graceful efficiency, cleared a path to the display of smartphones without seeming to push anybody out of the way. Kelly was again impressed how the other fairgoers, including aliens, somehow failed to react to the presence of the queen and her party as anything out of the ordinary. Then she saw a Grenouthian who was looking at them and holding a smartphone in front of one eye like an immersive camera.

"I think we're going to be on the Grenouthian news," she whispered to Joe.

"It doesn't seem to bother the queen, and I'm sure her bodyguards spotted the bunny before you did," he replied. "I have to admit that she's nothing like I expected for the leader of the Council of Queens."

"No, she's very nice," Kelly whispered.

"I heard that," Queen Asiedu said over her shoulder without turning her head. "Would anybody know how many eBucks are in a Stryx cred?"

"A little more than five," Joe replied immediately.

"Then I'm a little less impressed by these smartphones than I was a moment ago. Seventy creds for a mid-priced model? I'm sure the Dollnicks could simulate everything you can do with one on a standard mini-tab for a tenth of the price." She sighed and nodded to one of her guards, who produced a programmable cred and passed it to the clerk. "I'll take one of each. Maybe one day they'll be collectible, which is more than you can say for the Dollnick knock-offs."

Behind the queen, Kelly stealthily removed the decorative Dollnick wristwatch she wore and slid it into her purse.

Eleven

"Are you working on a new avatar?" Fenna asked. "I can't believe how many orders you get."

Mike tapped the current palette at the edge of the oversized Dollnick artist's tab with the stylus in his left hand to choose a new brush color. "I never even listed myself anywhere—it's all word of mouth," he told her proudly. "My dad sent the first few people to me, and with visor conferencing taking off, I get more jobs than I can accept."

"Are you keeping up with your homework? After studying so hard to start at the Open University in the same class as me it would be a shame if you dropped out."

"My mom would never let me—she'd take away my tab. Besides, it's the first week of class. How could I be behind?"

Aisha's daughter was about to answer when a young Verlock entered the lost-and-found and shuffled slowly towards the counter on which Mike was sitting cross-legged while working on his tab.

"Can I help you?" Fenna asked.

"Not – sure," the Verlock said in a voice that the girl's implant imparted with a deep note of despair. "Lost – detector."

"Can you give me any details, or do you have a picture? We make holographic catalog entries of all the items brought in, and if you have a picture, I can enter it in the system to search for a match."

The Verlock thought for a moment and then looked hopeful. "Mother – captured – image – to – send – grandfather. I'll – go – home – and – get – it."

"No, wait," Fenna said as the young Verlock turned and began to shuffle off. "This is my first day of work and you're the only client who I didn't help. If you go home, my shift may be over before you return. Can you describe the detector, or tell me when you noticed it was missing?"

"Standard – neutrino – detector – modified – with – Kygers – shroud. "Passive – experiment, I – only – checked – trap – once – a – cycle."

"So it may have been missing for more than a month." The girl turned to look up at the racking behind the counter that contained the most recent items brought into the lost-and-found. "But then again, it might have just come in today."

"Let him check the shelves," Mike suggested. "The way you explained it, everything brought in during the last cycle will be in the front-facing units."

"But I can't allow anybody who doesn't work here behind the counter," Fenna said.

"I – will – not – break – rules," the Verlock told them sternly. "I – will – look – from – here." He took several minutes shuffling down the full length of the long counter with his eyes on the shelving units, but he failed to spot the detector. "I – will – go – home – for – image – and – return."

"You can't have your mother send it to your tab?" Mike asked.

The alien's leathery features crinkled up in horror. "Verlocks – don't – tell – parents – what – to – do."

Fenna didn't try to stop the Verlock from exiting a second time, but she let out a sad sigh. "When I went to orientation for lost-and-found work-study students, the Horten girl who showed us how everything worked said that it's good luck if you help every client recover their lost item on your first day. Now I'm fourteen for fifteen, and we'll be gone before he gets back."

"I came for your last half-hour, and I just got here a few minutes ago," Mike said. "If he runs to the lift tube and—you're right. But maybe his detector isn't here. Would that still count as a failure?"

"Pretty much everybody asks the station librarian for help when they lose something, and Libby wouldn't have sent him here if it isn't on the shelf."

"Do you want me to help you look? I know you're afraid of heights, so I can go up on that platform thing and check the high shelves."

"You can't come on this side of the counter without special permission," Fenna reminded him. "Do you want to get me fired?"

"I doubt anybody has ever been fired from a work-study job in the history of the Open University," Mike said. "Besides, I might want to work here one day, so it would almost be like training."

The teenage girl ignored him and went to the easy-round holographic cataloging device at the end of the counter to address it from within the voice interface radius. "Do we have any Verlock neutrino detectors on the shelves?"

"Forty-three," the artificial voice replied.

"Were any brought in during the last cycle?"

"Negative."

"You see," Mike said. "It doesn't count as a failure on your part because it's not here. The Verlock probably forgot where he left it."

"I've never heard of a Verlock with a bad memory. Libby?"

"Yes, Fenna," the Union Station librarian responded immediately.

"Is there any way to find out what happened to the neutrino detector the Verlock who just came in was looking for?"

"When young Fwryn arrives home he will find the detector on the kitchen table. The family is playing a prank on him to celebrate his acceptance to a prestigious science academy on their homeworld."

"Verlocks have a sense of humor?" Mike asked skeptically. "I was on *Let's Make Friends* with Krolyohne for two years and she never even told a joke."

"Yes, she did," Fenna said. "She told math jokes, but they were all so advanced that Spinner was the only one who got them."

"I forgot about that. Can I go behind the counter, Libby?"

"Do you have a compelling reason or are you just curious?" the Stryx station librarian replied.

"If I see something cool, I'd be more likely to take a work-study job here," Mike said.

"Given your earnings from creating custom avatars, I find that highly unlikely. And Fenna's relief just exited the lift tube."

"But my shift isn't up for another twenty minutes," Fenna protested.

"It's traditional for lost-and-found work-study students to relieve each other early," Libby explained.

"My trainer told me, but I thought that meant ten minutes. That means I was late."

"I'm sure Lorx understood."

A rail-thin Dollnick, who probably weighed half of what he eventually would when he reached maturity in a century or two, entered the lost-and-found and headed directly for the section of the counter that hinged up to admit employees.

"Krus," the alien introduced himself. "Am I early enough? It's my first day and I wasn't sure."

"Mine too, and you're fine," Fenna said. She retrieved her shoulder bag from the cubby designated for personal items and double-checked that she had replaced the student tab she'd had out to do homework earlier in the shift. "The Drazen on the shift before me cataloged all of the lost items in today's bin so you'll have plenty of time to study."

Krus wilted a little. "I finished all of my homework before I came, but I guess I can check all of my answers again and get a jump on my senior project."

"Aren't you a freshman?"

"Yes, but the early Dollnick gets the Sheezle bug."

Fenna couldn't think of any reason to contradict the alien, so she slung her bag over her shoulder and followed Mike out of the lost-and-found. "Thanks again for coming to visit me on my first day," she told him. "I'm sorry you didn't have enough time to get any work done."

"I wasn't drawing an avatar," he said, and then his ears turned pink, and he began walking faster.

"I can tell when you're drawing by the way you move the stylus," Fenna said. "What were you doing then?"

"Just fooling around."

"Let me see."

"I already put my tab away."

"What are you talking about? It's folded up there in the belt holder for a regular student tab."

"I'll show you if you come to Bitters with me," Mike said impulsively.

"What's Bitters?" Fenna asked.

"It's a new coffee shop in the Little Apple opened by some people from Bits who didn't want to live on Flower. They've got a lot of old computer parts on display and it's pretty cool."

They stopped in front of the lift tube and Fenna looked up at Mike, who was taller than her despite being a year younger. "Are you asking me on a date?"

"I'm just offering to buy you a tea or something to celebrate your first day at the lost-and-found," Mike said, though his ears began to color again. "You don't have to come."

"Bitters," Fenna told the lift tube as they entered. "I didn't say I wouldn't go. I'm just trying to find out if I can tell people we're dating. A guy in my Horten Studies class asked if I wanted to do a field trip with him this weekend to see a band."

"How old is he?" Mike asked, sounding a bit panicked.

"I don't know, maybe a year or two older than me. It's his first year. You know how you're younger than most of the students because Libby's experimental school let us learn at our own pace."

"What did you tell him?"

"I'd have to check with my boyfriend first." Fenna laughed at Mike's obvious look of relief. "Are you embarrassed by the idea of dating an older woman?"

"You're not a woman, you're a teenager, just like me," Mike retorted as the doors slid open just in time for a pair of middle-aged women who were waiting for the capsule to be amused by his remark. "You never used to say things like that."

"Because we were just kids in Libby's school, but we're university students now. Dating isn't anything to be embarrassed about."

"I don't get why you have to take stupid Horten Studies anyway," Mike said, and then his face lit up. "You know, you can drop and add in the first two weeks without any penalty. Isn't that your Tuesday/Thursday course? You should take Intro to Industrial Design with me."

"Horten Studies isn't stupid, and I'm way ahead from talking with Marilla all the time. I even know a few hundred words in Horten, though I can't pronounce half of them because it hurts my throat."

"That's even more reason you don't need to take Horten Studies. You know it all already."

"There's a lot more to the Hortens, to all of the species, than you learned on *Let's Make Friends,*" Fenna said. "I've picked up a little in Mac's Bones from Marilla and all of the aliens who come around to see the ambassador, but it's not the same as a course of study. I don't know what I want to do when I'm older, so I signed up for courses that interest me. The admin registered me for the Tunnel Network Culture track because that's the only major that included all my choices. Maybe I'll end up working for the Grenouthian network, just like my mother."

"There it is," Mike said, barely touching Fenna's shoulder to turn her toward the entrance of Bitters. "Have you told your mom that you want your own show?"

The girl stopped dead and stared at Mike. "Are you crazy? I meant doing research or something. For everybody in front of the immersive cameras, there's probably a hundred more behind them and in the booth, the offices, and all the other jobs at the network."

"I remember the alien kids from my two years on *Let's Make Friends,* and the Grenouthian assistant director who was always yelling at us, but that's about it."

"You don't remember my mom?" Fenna asked as they entered the café.

"I don't have to remember your mom because I still know her," Mike explained. "I keep expecting to see one of the other cast members in the Open University cafeteria, but it hasn't happened yet."

"What kind of wallpaper is that? It looks three-dimensional."

"It's real recycled bricks. They imported them from Earth. Let's sit in the corner at that table with the candle in the glass thing."

"What's that weird noise?" Fenna asked as she followed Mike to the table.

"You mean the music? I asked the last time I was here, and the guy at the counter said it was a mix tape like I should understand what that was. He said that all the cooperative members bring their favorite music for their shifts."

"So it's a cooperative, but I meant the other—there," she said, as an oddly muted blaring sound could be heard over the acoustic guitar.

"Oh, that's from the window," Mike said, pointing at a large display panel on the wall that was playing a street scene from Earth's past. "Every once in a while, some text comes up and tells when and where it was recorded. Last time the window was showing some place called Copenhagen from almost two hundred years ago."

"Pretty cool. Is there a menu or do we order from the counter?"

"Just wait for a minute," Mike said with a grin.

"Then show me your tab," Fenna demanded. "You promised."

Mike grumbled a little, but he pulled out the Dollnick artist's tab and unfolded it so it had four times the area of a standard student's tab. Then he swiped it to life, hesitated for a moment, and passed it to the girl, adding, "It's not finished yet."

"It's me working in the lost-and-found! But you were only there for like ten minutes, and we were talking the whole time."

"All the avatars I'm doing are from images people send me over the Stryxnet, so I'm getting good at sort of converting them into vector art. I snapped a picture of you when I came in, ran it through a couple of effects, and then I started customizing it. The trick to making good avatars for the visor conferencing system is to minimize the vectors required without losing the personality."

"I knew you were good at it, but that's more me than the me that I see in the mirror," Fenna enthused. "Can you animate it so I can see myself talking?"

"When it's finished," Mike said. "I'll send it to you, and then I'll borrow a couple of visors from my dad's office so we can meet in virtual reality, and you can really see what it's like."

"I'll see what you look like, not me."

"They have mirrors in virtual reality."

"You don't have to—what is that?" Fenna interrupted herself, pulling her feet up onto her chair like she had just seen a mouse.

"That's a twenty-first-century Earth waiter bot," Mike said as the robot that looked vaguely like a three-drawer filing cabinet rolled up to the table. The top drawer had a sort of a face, with two low-profile cameras for eyes and a thin rectangular speaker grid for a mouth.

"May I take your order?" a male voice asked.

"Is there a menu?" Fenna asked Mike.

"I have a menu," the robot declared. The middle drawer slid open and an arm brandishing a printed menu laminated in clear plastic popped out like a jack-in-the-box. "Do you require more than one minute to order? If so, I will return."

"House coffee for me," Mike said. "Black, no sweetener."

"I'll have a Masala chai," Fenna said as soon as she spotted it on the menu. "And we'll split a brownie. I'll pay for it, Mike."

"No way," the teenager said as the bot spun around and headed off. "I invited you and it's my treat. Besides, I earn a lot more than you do. You wouldn't believe what people are willing to pay for an avatar that doesn't make them look like a cartoon ghost in business meetings."

"I can see where professionals would want to avoid that. But was that robot real? Were people building artificially intelligent waiter bots on Earth before the Stryx came?"

"They aren't artificial intelligence, it's just speech recognition," Mike said. "I've been learning about old-fashioned computer programming because I have to follow some rules for my avatars to look right when they're moving. The waiter bot is just following a decision tree with preprogrammed responses."

"I can't believe how much a week at the Open University has improved your vocabulary," Fenna teased. "This must be the first time in our lives that you haven't said 'stuff' at least once every five seconds."

"One of my avatar clients told me that I did professional work but that I talked like a kid. At first, I was so angry that I almost turned her down when she asked for a quote to do avatars for her employees. Then I realized that she wasn't trying to insult me, so I started listening more carefully to how the adults I respect talk, and I'm trying to imitate them."

"What about the woman? Did you do the job?"

"I raised my price ten percent," Mike said and broke into a wide smile. "And once I started thinking more about what I wanted to say, I realized that the words were in me the whole time, I just hadn't been using them."

"You probably worried that you'd sound too smart," Fenna said. "So how did you find this place? Another one of your clients?"

"Libby told me about it. I asked her if there was a place I could go to work on my avatars when things were too busy at home. I thought she would find me an empty classroom, but she said that artists and writers sometimes benefit from anonymous company."

"I don't know what that is."

"When I'm at home and Grace or Queenie is doing something to get my attention, I can't ignore them—especially Queenie, because ignoring a Cayl hound is never a good idea," Mike said. "But I also have trouble working or studying if I'm completely isolated, like in one of the carrels with the acoustic suppression fields at the Open University library. Anonymous company is between the two extremes. People are coming and going, and I catch bits of conversation that might make me think, but I can just as easily filter it out because it's not aimed at me."

Fenna nodded her understanding. "Sometimes I feel that way myself, like I want to be around people, but not people who I have to talk to."

The robotic waiter returned with their order and placed the two drinks and the brownie on the table with a mechanical arm. "Will there be anything else?" it inquired.

"All set for now," Mike said.

The robot pivoted about and headed for a table where a couple of Drazens had just sat down.

"You didn't pay," Fenna said.

"On the way out," Mike told her. "The robot runs a tab and sends it to the register."

"I think I might come here myself to do homework sometime. There are a lot of distractions at home, and I don't like the study carrels either."

"Just remember that you already have a boyfriend if anybody asks."

Twelve

"Better, but you're almost a quarter-cred high per item on your profit projections," Jeeves told Dorothy. "At the volume we're talking, that adds up to more than your annual salary."

"But I included everything this time, even the new wellness fee that Flower tacked onto her price schedule to pay for employees to eat out somewhere nice once a week. How come we don't do that?"

"When's the last time you paid for anything on an employee outing?"

"That's because we always go LARPing, and those outings are more work than relaxation," Dorothy pointed out. "Myst is always thinking about her next set of epic jewelry, and Jyndal is busy trying to figure out how bags-of-holding function in LARPing space, not to mention whatever other magic tricks Baa's been teaching her. We need to go somewhere where the music isn't an ominous warning that monsters are about to attack. I haven't danced in ages."

"So pay for yourselves the next time you go LARPing, and if you find the missing quarter-cred, we'll talk about a night of dancing," Jeeves said, and he began floating toward the door of the breakroom. "How is Richard enjoying being a beta tester for the new Alt daycare?"

"He's talking more, and he hasn't screamed for grandma in weeks, but I miss having him in the office."

"Are you busy?" Dietro asked, sticking his head in the door of the breakroom.

"Jeeves was just giving me a hard time about my profit projections. He says I'm almost a quarter-cred high."

"Did you include packing materials? Just because they end up in the recycling bin doesn't mean that they're free."

"Packing materials," Dorothy said triumphantly. "You owe us an employee outing, Jeeves."

"I said we'd talk about it, but right now I don't have time," the young Stryx said. "And the orders from the New World's Fair are coming in faster than either of your projections, so you'll need to coordinate with Flower's people if we're going to keep up with our delivery promises."

"That's part of why I wanted to talk to you, but we'll get on it," Dietro said. "The other reason is I need to take the rest of the day off afterward and I want to borrow Jyndal."

"More mug shots?" Dorothy asked.

"They aren't criminals, they're actors and extroverts. If I can't figure out a way to spot better magical talent in a hurry, all of the time I put into developing *Mage Search* for the Grenouthian network will be wasted."

"You'll have to clear it with Baa," Jeeves said. "SBJ Fashions pays Jyndal's salary, but she's officially Baa's apprentice. Good luck with the holoconference."

"If—" Dietro began, but the Stryx had vanished with barely a sound, and they heard the main door to the office sliding closed. "He always runs off when I'm about to ask him for a favor with Baa."

"He was already running off when you arrived," Dorothy told the Vergallian. "Besides, he said you have to ask Baa about Jyndal yourself."

"I can do that, it's asking for Geb's help that makes me nervous. The network will pay him a finder's fee for spotting sentients with magical talent if he'll work for the show as a consultant."

"You want to hire Baa's cat?"

"He doesn't belong to her, and you don't know how desperate I'm getting. I put over five hundred hours into *Mage Search* in the last year and I don't have a fallback plan for impressing Affie's family."

"Why not ask Jeeves for a promotion?" Dorothy suggested. "With Shaina and Brinda stepping back, you could be vice president of marketing or something like that."

"I could be president with a salary of a hundred thousand creds a cycle and that wouldn't impress a royal Vergallian," Dietro said. "I'd still be working for two Humans, a Stryx, and a Terragram mage."

"And working for the Grenouthians is better?"

"I'm the show creator and co-producer, with points in the production. It's completely different."

"I wish I understood how aliens keep score," Dorothy muttered to herself. "Do you want to get the Flower thing out of the way?"

"Contact her and open a holoconference," Dietro said over his shoulder as he headed back out of the breakroom. "I'm going to run and get my tab."

"Libby? Can you ping Flower and ask if Julie is available for a holoconference?"

"You'll need your virtual reality visors," the station librarian replied.

"What for?" Dorothy asked. "I know you gave Flower unlimited bandwidth."

"She's insisting on conducting business through the visors to support the programmers from Bits on board who adapted them for the Stryxnet."

"Isn't that kind of artificial, like if everybody in the galaxy agreed to limit themselves to the technology of some primitive species for the sake of a level playing field?"

"I approve of Flower's decision," Libby told her. "An unfortunate side effect of our compelling Earth to join the tunnel network was that your technical progress came to almost a complete halt when your engineers and scientists learned that the gap between their capabilities and those of the least advanced tunnel network species were insurmountable in the near term. We protected a few of your key technologies from alien competition, but ultimately, a period of adjustment was unavoidable."

"Flower forcing people who work with her to use obsolete technology is supposed to help Earth?" Dorothy asked skeptically. "The visors are still piggybacking on the Stryxnet, which is beyond any of the tunnel network species."

"It's not the technology itself that's important, it's the willingness to build on what you know. The people who moved to Bits forty years ago in an attempt to preserve what was left of humanity's computing culture were on the right track. The only way for you to move forward as a technological species is to continue building on your own foundations."

Dorothy frowned. "Are you saying that my using Gem nanofabric for fittings and Verlock technology in dancing shoes is hurting us? That my dad's fixing and selling alien ships all these years is keeping humanity from developing our own ships?"

"No, but there's a reason we normally wait for species to develop interstellar travel before inviting them to join the tunnel network," Libby said. "We regard Earth as an experiment in progress."

"I brought you ankle controllers this time," Dietro said, returning to place a box with a virtual reality headset and four accessory controllers on the table and sliding it to Dorothy.

"How are you walking around with the visor on?" she asked him. "Did the conference already begin?"

"It's got cameras for a real-world mode that allow the visor to display a ghostly version of what you'd be seeing if you weren't wearing it. Sort of like the ambient sounds mode for audio that blends what you hear in virtual reality with what your ears would pick up without the headset covering them. Choose the visor icon to access the local settings when you put it on."

Dorothy put on the headset, navigated to settings, and selected the camera icon with practiced eye movements. The breakroom immediately reappeared, though there was something off about the colors and resolution, but she quickly adjusted enough to be able to put the controllers on her wrists and ankles without fumbling around. "It's kind of like working with a heads-up display overlay, but different," she commented.

"You can link the headset's controls to your implant if you prefer," Dietro told her.

"Did you ping Flower yet, Libby?" Dorothy asked.

"I just opened a virtual reality conference channel and Julie will be with you in a minute," the Stryx librarian replied.

"Switch over," Dietro said. "We're live, and this is worth seeing."

Dorothy navigated back to the menu, chose the visor icon, and deselected the camera. She immediately found herself on a virtual reality version of Flower's light industrial deck surrounded by aisles of cartoonish treadle sewing machines that seemed to go on forever. There must have been several hundred people at work sewing, mostly women wearing modest dresses that were favored by the old Way movement, but also a few dozen of Flower's permanent inhabitants, including a handful of men.

"We can't be selling that many dresses," she said to Dietro.

"Don't forget Flower is producing her own lines of work clothes and formalwear," the Vergallian sales manager reminded her. "She seems willing to leave high fashion to us for the time being."

"But what are all these people doing in our virtual reality conference? Does Flower have them all wearing visors?"

A young woman who appeared to be in the middle months of pregnancy suddenly popped into view right in front of Dorothy, reminding the EarthCent ambassador's daughter that she wasn't really visiting on Flower, and the whole meeting was taking place in the hardware of the headsets. The newcomer glanced around, sighed, and the busy factory scene was suddenly replaced by a typical conference room.

"Flower's latest employment project," Julie explained. "She's hired a whole team of artists from Bits to start creating virtual reality settings for all her business ventures. The scenes are visually compelling, but they aren't live, which can lead to awkward conversations."

"I'm working on it," the Dollnick artificial intelligence interjected.

"But doesn't all of the extra detail start using up the bandwidth that we're supposed to be saving by shifting from holoconferencing to virtual reality?" Dorothy asked.

"Not as much as you'd expect," Flower said. "The visors track your eye movements and only fill in the detail for the center of your vision. The servers are multiples of magnitudes faster than anything you had on Earth a century ago, which makes new usage cases for the visors possible."

"But I'm sure you didn't ping us all the way from Union Station to talk about computer technology," Julie said. "What can Flower Apparel do for you?"

"Our booth in the Human Empire pavilion at the New World's Fair is generating as many orders for bespoke dresses as all of our current franchises combined," Dietro said. "We've been giving you practically all of that work, and we're concerned that your turnaround time may start to creep up."

"I don't expect any problems as long as you don't double again in the next week."

"They're running full out at the booth with six nanofabric fitting stations, and we'd need more space to sell more, assuming the demand held up. What took us by surprise is that customers who visit a franchisee's boutique normally order a single dress per fitting, but at the fair they're averaging almost two and a half."

"Probably because most fair visitors have traveled a long way to get there while the franchises operate as local businesses in their communities," Dorothy added.

"Then you can rest assured that our production will meet your demand," Julie said. "Flower has a whole team of mechanics building new treadle sewing machines, and we've started recruiting stitchers from tech-ban worlds."

"What will you do with them all when the world's fair is over and demand collapses?"

Julie laughed out loud, and the avatar showed her teeth as perfect little rectangles of ivory. "Flower will never run out of work for stitchers. She's already plotting to move into hazmat suits and school uniforms."

"We're rapidly expanding the franchise network, so save some production capacity for us," Dietro said hastily. "My last projection indicates that our presence at the fair will more than double our franchise base over the next six months. There may be a dip between the end of the fair and the new franchisees getting up to speed, but I'll bet that a year from now our volume is higher than today."

"A year from now I should be back from maternity leave," Julie said. "I'm supposed to find a temporary replacement for myself if you happen to know anybody who doesn't mind getting bossed around by an opinionated Dollnick AI."

"You might want to work on that job description," Dorothy said. "Your avatar looks great, by the way."

"Yours too. Was there anything else today?"

"I'm sorry, we must have interrupted something by pinging you without notice," Dietro said. "That's all I had."

The Vergallian's avatar disappeared from the virtual conference room in a swirling tornado of flame.

"Wow, I've never seen that one before," Julie said. "He must have paid a pretty cred for it."

"I'm sorry about dragging you into a meeting over nothing," Dorothy said. "Drink plenty of milk."

Dietro had already left the breakroom by the time Dorothy removed her virtual reality gear, but she found him a minute later in the design room trying to cajole Baa into giving Jyndal the afternoon off.

"She's been enchanting rings of plus one all morning and she shouldn't be alone," Baa was telling Dietro.

"I'll be with her the whole time."

"You don't count. Jyndal still has control issues, and you aren't capable of detecting an unconscious flare on her part, much less stopping it."

"If you come, I'll—"

"No," Baa cut him off.

"How about Geb?" Dietro tried. "Can he control magical leakage or whatever?"

"Ask him."

"I can't even see him."

"He's on top of Myst's 3D design station staring at you like he wonders what Vergallians taste like."

"Geb," Dietro addressed the empty space above the workstation that the Gem part-timer used to model jewelry. "How would you like to visit the Grenouthian studio with me and Jyndal and look through some holographic candidate applications for my *Mage Search* show? I can pay for your time."

"Now he's looking at you like he wonders if Vergallians have brains," Baa reported. "What makes you think anybody can spot magical talent by looking at a hologram?"

"But there has to be some way of doing it," Dietro said. "How can you be sure if he doesn't try?"

"I never thought that working here could get any weirder, but it has," Dorothy said. "Is Geb really there, Baa, or are you just fooling around?"

"Party pooper," the Terragram mage said. "What about you, Jyndal? Do you want to go with Dietro to look at audition holograms?"

"What about flares?" the girl asked. "When Ofer came and took me out for lunch the other day, a bunch of the people eating in the café had trouble with their tabs that I think might have been my fault."

"You can't rush to blame yourself for every technical glitch that happens when you're around," Dorothy said. "It could just have easily been local interference from some alien technology carried by a tourist."

"Except I saw a few of the screens and they were all frozen on an image of a silver ring," Jyndal said. "I'd been enchanting silver rings of dark vision all morning." Her upper body suddenly swayed, as if she had momentarily lost her balance, and then she reached up and began stroking the invisible cat on her shoulder. "I guess it's okay to try if Geb wants to come."

"Two hours," Baa said, holding up two fingers. "Not the whole afternoon. I want you to start on another bag-of-holding when you get back, Jyndal, so don't waste your energy trying to scry holograms. You can't force magic through technology any more than you can power a draft animal with a fusion generator."

"I thought magic was just technology that we don't understand," Dorothy said.

"You can say that about anything you don't understand without making it true."

Dietro lowered the finger that he'd been pointing at his ear and shook his head in disappointment. "I pinged the studio to tell them we're coming, but my co-producer's reservation got bumped by an active show. We can reschedule for tomorrow."

"Why not run the holograms in our breakroom?" Dorothy suggested. "We have a projection system."

The Vergallian brightened up and pointed at his ear again, and this time he signed off with a nod. "He sent me the access key, but it will probably take me a minute to get it running. See you all in the breakroom."

Jyndal set to work trying to convince Baa to participate, though ultimately it was Dorothy's reminder that the Terragram mage was in for twenty-five percent of Dietro's cut that persuaded her. Geb lapped up a saucer of cream to get in the mood, manifesting as a jet-black cat in the process, and then the holographic auditions began playing.

"Yorf," a Drazen male surrounded by hundreds of candles and sitting cross-legged on the floor of a cave introduced himself. "From an early age I've had the ability to levitate objects using only the power of my mind." He tossed a coin on the rock floor and stared at it intently. At first, it began to vibrate, the edges lifting from the floor and dropping back, and then it slowly drifted upward, the strain showing on Yorf's face.

"Iron coin being attracted by a transparent magnet suspended by a thread from the tip of his tentacle," Baa said in a bored voice. "Next."

"Skip," Dietro instructed the projection system, bringing up a woman in her twenties who was tattooed like a Horten pirate.

"Adele," she said with a sneer as if the audition format requirements offended her. She spread a deck of Tarot cards on a leather-topped table and stared into the camera that was capturing the front view for the hologram. "I see the future, and I'm certified by the joint EarthCent-Verlock Bureau of Tourism program."

Geb slapped the now clean saucer with his paw to produce a clatter and hissed at the hologram, which froze.

"Geb isn't impressed by statistically significant forecasting," Baa interpreted. "He says you can either read the future or you can't. Having a feeling that lets you choose the winning color in roulette more often than random chance is a good way to get banned from a casino, but it's not the same as knowing for sure."

"Wait," Dietro said. "It may not be up to your standards, but it's something. Did any of you get an impression from the hologram that tells you she's lying?"

Jyndal shook her head, and Baa pointed at the certificate on the wall over Adele's shoulder.

"I hate to agree with Baa, but a bunch of people who can defy the odds sitting around playing guessing games wouldn't make for much of a show," Dorothy said.

"Doesn't it mean they have some aptitude?" Dietro persisted.

"What's less than a modicum?" Baa asked rhetorically. "A smidgen?"

"But anything is better than nothing. Maybe I should have started with the testing program for Human fortune tellers. The only species I'm confident I have enough contestants lined up for is Verlocks."

"What about sentients who get banned from casinos?" Jyndal asked. "Wouldn't that be a good place to start?"

"There are millions of ways to cheat at gambling, including all sorts of technology from more advanced species. That's why tunnel network casinos hire Thark consultants to keep their games straight."

"Then you should talk to them. Ofer knows their ambassador, and he said something about the Tharks keeping extensive records about gamblers from all over the galaxy who defy the odds. He says that the ambassador is super smart and writes books when he isn't doing diplomacy."

"Makes book," Dietro said. "It's not the same thing.

Thirteen

"Hey, Bob," Daniel greeted the Galactic Free Press reporter. "If you're here to see Judith, she ran out to bring something to the Fillinduck embassy, and she took the baby with her."

"I'll just leave this on her desk then, but I'm here to see you," Bob said, placing a takeout salad container on his wife's display desk. "I came through the Little Apple on the way, and I know Judith didn't have time to make her lunch this morning because our eldest was having a bad hair day."

"Don't take this the wrong way, but when the senior reporter for the Galactic Free Press on Union Station says he's here to see me, I start to worry. Why don't you come back to my office and we'll discuss it. I was just over here to talk to Ofer."

Bob glanced at the door to Kelly's office. "You kept your office on the other side of the conference room even though you're standing in for Ambassador McAllister while she's on Earth?"

"Saves moving twice," Daniel said, leading the reporter across the lobby. "And most of the aliens we deal with don't differentiate between CoSHC, EarthCent, and the Human Empire at this point. Do you want to stop for a coffee?" he asked as they entered the conference room.

"Have you ever met a journalist who didn't?" Bob responded. "Besides, I was up half the night at that Gambling Commission meeting. Ofer did a good job standing in for you."

"The Thark ambassador seems to enjoy Ofer's company, and Ofer is strangely enthusiastic about participating in the commission. I can't help wondering if all the reading he did about collectivism while growing up is coming to the surface."

"Communists were big gamblers?"

"I was thinking that they liked staying up all night for meetings where they'd make the decisions for everybody who couldn't attend," Daniel said as he poured the reporter a mug of coffee in the kitchenette. "The proletariat had to be in bed so they could get to work in the morning." He checked the day-old bakery box on the counter. "We may as well sit at the conference table since we're already here. Donut?"

"Watching my weight," Bob said, patting his belly. "I've been spending way too much time sitting with all of these new commissions EarthCent is participating in."

"Yeah, and I'm more than a little suspicious that the other ambassadors waited for Kelly's temporary absence to spring them on us. The timing was just a little too coincidental."

"Do you have any proof?"

"Off the record?"

Bob held up three fingers in the Station Scout's pledge.

"Between you and me, I noticed a few years ago that the other ambassadors started scheduling most of the meetings that Kelly attends on our clock," Daniel said. "It's not a major inconvenience for them since they're all on different length days and can go much longer without sleep than we can, but being able to hold meetings on your own clock is the main perk for committee chairs, and the same applies to commissions."

"Do you think they knew ahead of time that Kelly would end up as EarthCent's acting president during the New World's Fair and they scheduled the new commissions accordingly?"

"I imagine their intelligence services saw it coming from a light year away, and I know that Srythlan, at least, worries about Kelly's health because he always asks me. He must have known how long the Historical Commission meetings would run and wanted to spare her."

"Interesting theory," Bob said. "I've noticed for some time now that Ambassador McAllister is slowing down, and it's possible the other ambassadors are hoping to keep her in place for the sake of continuity until the Human Empire takes over. And I've heard her say that she doesn't approve of gambling."

"I've heard her say it at poker games," Daniel said with a grin as he sat down at the conference table across from the journalist. "But I don't imagine any of this has to do with why you came to see me."

"I almost forgot about that. The Alt who negotiated the original Earth Two agreement is back on Union Station again, and he's been visiting all the alien embassies."

"Methan? I wonder why he would be making the rounds himself rather than sending Affie. I thought the Alts were very happy with the arrangement for the Vergallians to supply contract queens."

Bob took a sip from his coffee before replying. "EarthCent Intelligence does a good job tracking interspecies business activity, which makes sense since that's their main focus. But when it comes to alien diplomatic moves, they tend to be at the back of the pack. I heard from a couple of my alien contacts that the Alts are interested in making Earth Two an open world."

"It already is an open world," Daniel said. "I'm pretty sure more humans are living there than Alts. Flower would know the exact numbers since she's transporting all the colonists."

"The agreement Samuel made with Methan is for a shared world. An open world would welcome all aliens willing to abide by the rules."

"To what end? Are the Alts hoping to dilute our presence with the other species? Do they have some complaint about the conduct of our colonists that they haven't been relaying to us through channels?"

"My sources didn't give a reason," Bob said. "The only thing they were certain of was that Methan was making inquiries about the ins and outs of running open worlds."

"They can't intend to open their homeworld to settlement, nobody does that, and I'm not aware of their owning any other habitable planets, other than Earth Two," Daniel said with a frown. "How reliable is your information?"

"It's from alien journalists. None of them are enthusiastic about sitting through long commission meetings, and I finally have enough standing in the profession to do some trading."

"Maybe it's so preliminary that Methan didn't want to bother their contract queen. Or—" he paused for a long moment, "maybe we have this completely backward. What if the Alts are interested in open worlds as alternative destinations for their people who are interested in seeing more of the tunnel network?"

"Colonist tourism?" Bob asked. "That seems a bit farfetched, and I don't remember hearing anything about population pressure on their homeworld. I thought the main reason they bought Earth Two was that the small continent was already terraformed with flora and fauna from Earth, plus they didn't want us to get there first and ruin it."

"That's just the thing," Daniel said. "The whole business with Earth Two wasn't something they had planned on, and when the opportunity to buy came up, they felt trapped into it. But don't forget they developed interstellar travel without any help, and they wouldn't have done that if they were xenophobic. They probably intended all along to take part in the broader galaxy on their own terms. Then they were blindsided by the fact that their ancient enemies, humans, had gotten here before them."

"I suppose that does make more sense than the idea they would be rushing to declare Earth Two an open world. Besides, until the population increases enough for a tunnel network connection, I can't see why any aliens would want to move there."

"Libby," Daniel said out loud. "Is Affie in her office?"

"She just returned from lunch," the Stryx librarian replied. "Do you want me to ask if she's available?"

"Yes. Tell her I'd like to drop by as soon as possible."

There was a brief pause, and then Libby said, "She's available now, but she has to attend an event for Ambassador Aleeytis in approximately a half hour."

"Tell her I'm on my way," Daniel said, picking up his coffee mug and heading for the kitchenette. "I want to get to the bottom of this now, and I'll let you know what I find out, off the record," he told Bob. "You're welcome to stay and wait for your wife."

"I'll do that," the reporter said. "And maybe I'll have a few words with Ofer."

Affie was waiting at the doors of the Vergallian embassy when Daniel arrived, and she turned him right around to reenter the lift tube.

"Did your other event get moved up?" he asked after she requested the park deck. "Is it one of those picnic-type things?"

"My office in the embassy isn't secure," she told him. "I'm not officially an employee so our intelligence people see me as fair game."

"Vergallian Intelligence is spying on you while you're representing the Alts?"

Affie made a face. "On the bright side, the Alts have nothing to hide and aren't competing with anybody, so whoever has to read through all of the transcripts must be bored silly."

"Thanks for the warning. I hope my visit doesn't get you in trouble with Aleeytis."

"Vergallian diplomats and intelligence types don't see eye to eye on most things. The ambassador was furious when she found out that our cultural attaché was spying on me, but she can't do anything about it."

The doors opened on a white pebble path that ran through a sculpted garden, a section of the park deck that Daniel had never visited. "This can't be the same place I take our Cayl hound for a run every night," he said.

"The lift tube delivered us to the section maintained by Vergallian volunteers. It's not off-limits to the other species, but it's way at the end of the station. There's a pretty thick hedgerow running around the circumference."

"I've seen that hedgerow. I thought it was the end of the deck."

"There's a gate, I think, but you'd have to walk all day to find it," Affie said. "So why did you want to see me right away?"

"I heard through the grapevine that Methan has been going around to all of the embassies asking about open worlds," Daniel said. "At first, I thought it meant they want to do something with Earth Two, but then it occurred to me that the Alts are interested in establishing colonies on the open worlds of other tunnel network species."

"I really can't say. Would you like me to arrange a meeting between the two of you?"

"He hasn't told you what he's planning?" Daniel asked in surprise.

"Of course he has, but I work for the Alts, not for Humans," Affie said patiently.

"Sorry. I'm used to Aabina, and now that she's been away for a few months with Kelly, I guess I mixed the two of you up in my mind. Sure, I'll take a meeting with Methan if he's willing, but perhaps we should keep it informal."

"Please explain your reasoning."

"Well, for one thing, I'm not sure what standing I have with the Alts when their deal is with the Human Empire and Methan is used to working directly with Samuel. For another, I have a sneaking suspicion that my source may have been played by his sources to try to bring about some result that I haven't figured out yet."

Affie leaned towards a bush covered with brilliant magenta flowers to sniff the fragrant blossoms. "That's pretty much what I suspected. If you don't mind a lot of background noise, we can see Methan right now. I pinged ahead when you said you were coming."

"What background noise?"

"He's currently observing at the new experimental daycare set up by the Alts. His daughter, Meena, was the one who suggested it."

"The Alts don't have any tradition of daycare facilities?"

"This one is mixed, for Alt and Human preschoolers," the Vergallian explained. "Meena worked for InstaSitter during previous stays on Union Station so she's training the Alt volunteers."

"Sure, if we won't be interrupting," Daniel said, hoping that the room wouldn't be full of screaming children. "Where is it located?"

"In a temporary space that I rented for them on the Vergallian deck. Don't mention that part to Methan—he thinks it was free."

"He's still not comfortable with the business aspects of the tunnel network?" Daniel asked as they reentered the lift tube.

"Vergallian deck," Affie told the capsule before replying. "Yes and no. Yes, he's still not comfortable with the whole concept of money, no, it doesn't prevent him from making rational decisions. One of the most remarkable things I've observed about the Alts while working for them is their willingness to make the best out of a bad situation."

"Sounds like they don't get any pleasure out of being sore losers. It's what keeps a lot of humans going."

"That's a reasonable way of putting it. Ofer is fascinated by the Alts and is always coming around asking me questions about them."

"If the Human Empire's relationship with the Alts ever progresses to the point of exchanging ambassadors, I'll recommend Ofer for the job," Daniel said with a laugh.

"Except I don't think he'll leave Union Station as long as his girlfriend is apprenticed to Baa. Have you met her?"

"I'm still employed by SBJ Fashions even though I'm never there," Affie said. "Dietro works with Jyndal almost every day. He says that she has made remarkable progress as a person in the last year after being isolated on a Verlock world throughout her teens."

"I've met her a few times at office parties but that's about it. My wife is putting all of her efforts into the *All Species Cookbook* these days, so she only goes by SBJ Fashions if there's some special reason, which doesn't happen often. I guess Dorothy and Dietro are managing."

"Sometimes I can't believe Dorothy is the same person I knew just ten years ago. I don't know if it was getting married and having children or just something about the Human maturation process, but she's gone from being a fashion-crazed teenager to a respectable and competent businesswoman."

"Ten years is a long time with us," Daniel said as he followed Affie onto the Vergallian deck. "What kind of temporary space did you find for the daycare?"

"The last business was a companion agency for travelers. I don't think Humans have anything similar these days, but you can think of companions as professional chaperones."

"Did they go under?"

"Under?" the Vergallian princess asked, glancing reflexively at the deck. "You mean did the business fail? I think you could say that they were victims of their own success. They burned through the local pool of available upper-caste Vergallians who were qualified enough for the job and poor enough to take it. I believe the office does a circuit of Stryx stations to soak up the refugee talent and then moves on."

"Vergallian refugees? Where do they come from?"

"The Empire of a Hundred Worlds. There are always succession battles going on somewhere, and most defeated royals would rather leave with their retainers than see a rival take over. We've largely eliminated those fights on Fleet worlds, but the empire is old-fashioned."

Daniel would have asked more questions about this rarely discussed facet of the tunnel network's most populous species, but they had reached the daycare, and Affie held a cautionary finger to her lips. Several large windows allowed pedestrian traffic in the corridor to look in, and EarthCent's associate ambassador found himself imagining a collection of threadbare royals sitting on a row of chairs waiting for a wealthy Vergallian family to hire them as a young woman's companion. Then his eyes focused on a toddler who seemed to be chasing several grown Alts around the room. Just as he recognized the two-year-old as Kelly's grandson, the door opened and Methan came out.

"I don't know how Meena does it," the Alt representative said as he offered Daniel a handshake. "I would have required at least three meditation breaks by now to remain calm."

"Is Richard the only child in the daycare?" Daniel asked.

Methan glanced through the window with a puzzled look, and then he shook his head. "The four Alt children are taking turns drawing on a blackboard just below the windows so they're out of view. Dorothy's son is currently the only Human in the program, but he makes up for his lack of numbers with his energy."

Affie politely hid her mouth with her hand and laughed. "That's one way of putting it. He's certainly giving those women a good workout."

"Is your daughter in the room?" Daniel asked. "I don't see Meena, but it's been over a year since we last met."

"She stepped out as an experiment," Methan said. "As a result, the trainees immediately became anxious. Either Richard sensed their weakness and is attacking, or he wants to touch them to let them know it's all right."

"Is Meena uncomfortable with Richard as well?"

"She thinks he's the most wonderful little boy ever and would adopt him if Dorothy allowed it. These days, Meena is having a hard time empathizing with her fellow Alts. I'm afraid that the aggressiveness training Affie gave her last year was almost too effective."

"It seems to have affected you as well if you're assigning blame to me," Affie said with another laugh. "Tell him why you wanted to meet, Associate Ambassador Cohan."

"I heard you've developed an interest in open worlds," Daniel said. "I couldn't help wondering if you were thinking in that direction about Earth Two, or if you were exploring opportunities for your people to live among aliens on well-established worlds. I also wondered if you have any thoughts about Earth being declared a Galactic Historical site."

Methan hesitated, and then he said, "Let me answer your second question first. While all Alts would like our heritage sites on Earth to be preserved, we don't have any expertise in such work, since Alt was a blank slate when the Stryx transported us there tens of thousands of years ago. I'm also unsure what Earth being declared a Galactic Historical site would entail, whether there would be any responsibilities or—" he glanced at Affie, "—outlays of capital required on our part."

"I'm a little uncertain about the whole process myself, as the commission has only met twice, and there are dozens of planets up for consideration," Daniel said. "We seem to spend most of our time planning site visits, which the ambassadors on the commission view as a perk. Do you want me to ask if you can participate?"

"Travel to Earth in the company of alien diplomats?" The Alt seemed genuinely surprised by the suggestion as if it was a possibility that had never occurred to him. "Their presence would offer a sort of a buffer," he said, speaking more to himself than to Daniel, "and Meena has been pestering us to take her to your New World's Fair. I'll think about it."

"It can't hurt for me to ask now to make sure it's a possibility," Daniel said. "And maybe you'd be interested in sitting in on a meeting. They're officially open to the public, though the ambassadors are old hands at scaring everybody off."

"They aren't open to genuine debate?" Methan asked, obviously bothered by the notion that the tunnel network ambassadors would prefer to conduct their business in private. "Do they have something to hide?"

"You have to remember that the audiences at debates on your homeworld and the audiences at public meetings on Stryx stations have little in common," Affie told him. "I think it would be a good idea for you to attend a few commission meetings just to get a feel for it if nothing else. As of a couple of cycles ago, there's also a Gambling Commission holding meetings on Union Station."

"Are they finally talking about ending the scourge of gambling?" Methan asked hopefully. "It was bad enough when we learned that all of the tunnel network species use money," he managed not to stumble over the unpalatable word, "as a medium of exchange, but when I heard that even the most advanced species often wager money on outcomes of chance, I almost despaired of the galaxy."

"Uh," Daniel said, trying to think of a way to break the news to the Alt, "the Gambling Commission is more about regulating existing activity than stamping it out. Most species view making bets as a form of entertainment."

Fourteen

"It's so strange for Verlocks to be late to anything," Kelly said to Joe as she scanned the broad entry plaza at the New World's Fair once again. "It's not like Aabina would have gotten lost, so they must have insisted on stopping somewhere."

"I'm surprised she hasn't called," Joe said.

"We agreed to start texting instead, so I could look through the old ones at the end of the day and copy anything important to remember in my notebook." Kelly took out her smartphone and checked the screen to see if she'd somehow missed a text notification. "What does 'update complete' mean?"

"Didn't you see the message yesterday about a new operating system update? I chose to install it immediately, but I think there was a message that it would install automatically within the next twenty-four hours otherwise."

"I thought it was spam. It's so hard to tell what's real and what isn't, and I didn't want to get hacked again." She followed the onscreen instructions to restart the phone, and a minute later, a series of texts from Aabina filled the screen. "They'll be here in another five minutes."

"What happened?" Joe asked.

"Aabina says that when Verlocks are traveling on alien worlds, they insist on settling their hotel bill every morning instead of running a tab. But there turned out to be an error in the bill, and the clerk wasn't able to fix it manually, so they had to talk to the manager and—" Kelly looked up from the long text, "—it turned out to be a software bug."

"Let me guess. Despite never having seen the reservation and billing system before, the Verlocks got caught up in debugging and fixed it."

"First, they had to bypass the security to get access to the hotel chain's servers, and then they fixed it. Aabina said it took them less than twenty minutes, and they insisted on paying the corrected bill, even though the manager wanted to comp their stay."

"Can't take Verlocks anywhere," Joe said with a chuckle. "I imagine they have to sit on their hands the whole time they're on Earth to keep from correcting all of our errors."

Colonel Davidson came out of the security office and asked, "Can I get you some folding chairs? You've been standing for quite a while."

"Thank you, Pam, but our party will be here in a few minutes. It's the Verlock emperor's grandson today, but he's traveling incognito with just a tutor and a bodyguard. I've been looking forward to their visit all week."

"Really? My own experience with Verlocks is limited, and I've been hoping to keep it that way. They talk so slowly that I find myself interrupting to guess what they're going to say next."

"The important thing is that they walk slowly," Kelly said. "Thanks to my new shoes and a few months of escorting groups around the fairgrounds, I can stay on my feet for hours. But I thought I was going to have a heart attack last week trying to keep up with the Grenouthian delegation, and the Dollnicks take such long strides."

"You must have seen even more of the exhibits than I have by this point," the colonel said. "Any favorites?"

"It's funny, but I've lived away from Earth since I was twenty, and I'd forgotten how different the people and cultures from around the world can be. We have specialty restaurants on Union Station, but the total human population is less than any of the big cities on Earth, so there's a limit to the variety. I suppose in another hundred thousand years, there will just be one flavor of humans who all speak and look pretty much the same."

"That's how it is with the aliens on Stryx stations, but when you visit their planets and get into the backwaters, there's more variety," Joe said, and then his head swung around. "Here they come. I've never seen a floater riding that low to the ground. The driver must have turned off the load adjustment to save on the batteries."

"I'll never forget the security briefing an EarthCent Intelligence agent came to give us about the different species before the fair opened," Pam said. "John explained that Verlocks are denser than any of the other tunnel network species and have tougher skins than some dragon variants. If the hologram he showed wasn't faked, the Verlocks like sitting in pools of boiling water."

"They prefer extreme environments, especially volcanically active worlds," Kelly told the head of fair security. "But they're also some of the nicest sentients on the tunnel network if you take the time to get to know them."

Aabina led the three Verlocks to the bypass gate at the security building and made the introductions. The emperor's grandson turned out to be in his early hundreds, finished with his schooling, but still too young by Verlock standards to marry. The tutor was a female, and easily the eldest of the trio, while something about the bodyguard reminded Joe of Ambassador Srythlan's assistant at the embassy on Union Station.

"So, Ernyad," Kelly addressed the emperor's grandson. "Is there any particular aspect of the fair you're interested in seeing?"

"Human – Empire," the Verlock pronounced slowly. "Can – visit – the – rest – on – our – own."

"How long do you plan to remain on Earth?"

"As – long – as – it – takes. Your – planet – is – intriguing."

"Thank you, I've never heard it described that way," Kelly said. She began moving along the familiar route to the Human Empire pavilion at about two-thirds of her normal walking pace, keeping a close eye on the Verlocks to see if they were struggling to keep up. "I heard you had some excitement at the hotel."

"Room – service – undercharged – us," Ernyad told her. "Three – for – two – margaritas – was – miscoded."

"I don't think I've ever offered a Verlock a margarita," Joe said. "Which flavor do you like?"

"Didn't – drink – them. Ordered – for – the – salt."

"Koshering – salt," the tutor added. "Excellent – crystal – size."

"You couldn't get room service to just bring you up some salt?"

"Not – on – menu."

"Oh, look," Kelly said, pointing at one of the food trucks that either rotated through the parking spots at the fair or were forced to leave every night and find a new spot every morning. "A peanut roaster. I don't know anything more addictive when they get the salt right."

The Verlocks changed course for the food truck without a word, and Aabina gave Joe a wink that suggested Kelly had just scored a diplomatic coup. After trying a sample, the emperor's grandson produced a sack the size of a pillowcase and asked the peanut vendor to fill it. While the surprised woman was shoveling peanuts into the sack with a scoop designed to fill little paper envelopes, a sad-looking teenager approached the group.

"Excuse me," he said to the tutor, possibly mistaking her for the matriarch of the trio. "I'm very hungry."

The bodyguard touched the translation pendant hanging around his thick neck to activate it and asked, "Why – are – you – hungry?"

"I think that—" Kelly began, but the emperor's grandson held up a hand to stop her.

"My parents paid for me to go to a private school in the city, but it closed and threw us all out on the street," the teen said. "I'm too ashamed to go back to our town after my parents sacrificed everything for me to study math. I want to go to the Verlock academy, but I don't have enough for—"

"That's enough of that," a gravelly voice interrupted, and the teen, who turned to flee, collided with an especially tough-looking Verlock wearing a laminated ID on a lanyard. "You're under arrest for charity fraud."

"Drynal?" the Verlock bodyguard asked, and the astonishment in his voice was apparent even via the echo Kelly and Joe heard from the still-active translation pendant. "What – are – you – doing – here?"

"Interspecies Police Operations Agency," the new Verlock said at a normal speaking cadence for humans. "The New York city-state authorized us to establish a flying squad to deal with charity scammers targeting tourists from our respective species. I've been following this one all morning."

"Are – you – sure – he's – lying?" the emperor's grandson asked. "Looks – skinny."

"They all look skinny," Drynal said. The teenager made a sudden attempt to break out of the Verlock's grip by biting the alien on the wrist, but if Drynal noticed, he didn't give any sign of it. "I'll take him to security and have him banned from the fair."

"Wait." Ernyad took one of the pre-filled little paper bags of peanuts from the vendor's counter and handed it to the teen. "In – case – he's – hungry."

"You knew that policeman?" Kelly asked the bodyguard after Drynal departed with the grifter.

"Trained – me. Knew – he – worked – with – ISPOA – but – not – that – he – was – on – Earth."

"He didn't seem to recognize the emperor's grandson."

"On – purpose, so – not – to – draw – attention," the bodyguard said.

Ernyad paid the vendor for the peanuts without questioning the price, and to Kelly's surprise, he held onto the sack rather than passing it to the bodyguard.

"Do you plan to carry that all day?" she asked the emperor's grandson. "I can call for somebody to take it back to your hotel room, or they could hold it in the security office."

"Not – necessary," the Verlock said. "Snacks. Try – some."

Even though she wasn't hungry, Kelly took a small handful of the still-warm freshly roasted peanuts crusted with salt. By the time they reached the Human Empire pavilion, she had to ask her husband to exchange places and walk next to the emperor's grandson because she couldn't stop eating.

"Is there a particular exhibition you want to visit in the Human Empire pavilion?" Joe asked for the sake of making conversation.

"I – want – you – to – introduce – me – to – your – son," the Verlock said. "Proper – to – pay – my – respects – to – first – emperor."

Joe shot Kelly a look before saying, "I'm sorry, but Samuel is at Human Empire headquarters on Flower. I can introduce you to Larry, the Minister of Trade."

"Told – pavilion – supports – visor – conferencing."

"Of course," Kelly said. "Aabina, can you run ahead and contact Flower so they're ready for us?"

"I'm not sure the visor screens can be adjusted far enough apart for Ernyad's pupillary distance," Aabina said apologetically. "Verlock heads are appreciably wider than most humanoids."

"We – will – modify," the tutor said confidently.

Aabina hurried ahead, in part to give herself time to dig up a technician's tool kit for the Verlocks, though she had no idea how they could modify a mass-produced headset. Fortunately, the Verlocks stopped for a few minutes to watch a nanofabric demonstration at the SBJ Fashions booth. Then they paused for twenty minutes to examine the smartphones on display and purchase three of the latest models to use while on Earth. By the time the party arrived at the visor conferencing booth, Kelly's Vergallian assistant had scrounged up an impressive array of tools, some carbon fiber chairs that wouldn't collapse under the weight of the Verlocks, and a folding table to serve as a workbench.

Ernyad and his tutor each spent a few minutes examining a headset, and after a brief consultation, the emperor's grandson took a screwdriver and began removing tiny screws from the inside of the visor.

"Do you have spares?" Kelly whispered to the young man who had been assigned to help them.

"More than you can imagine," he replied. "When Flower visited last year and bought up all the new-old-stock from warehouses where it had been abandoned when the Stryx opened Earth, she didn't realize that there were several hundred thousand more headsets in a container carrier beached at one of the ship graveyards in India. International shipping trade fell apart overnight with the introduction of floating Dollnick container carriers that didn't require port facilities."

"And they're still good after a century?"

"The batteries all needed replacing, but those old shipping containers were made of steel, and the bubble retail packaging for the individual headsets is nearly indestructible. That's what makes it so bad for the environment."

"My – hands – too – large," Ernyad said to Aabina when he finished removing the screws. "Could – you?"

The Vergallian princess reached into the visor with her slender fingers and found the curved display screens for each eye were now loose and easily removed from the headset. By this time the tutor had located a coat hanger and bent it into the shape of oversized glasses. The two Verlocks worked together smoothly to set the display screens into the frames and string the fiber optic cables into the interface unit they removed from the cannibalized headset.

"It looks like they know what they're doing," the young man from the booth said to Kelly. "Have either of you ever used the visors?"

"Just once to try it," Kelly admitted. "As an ambassador, I had free access to full holoconferencing, so there wasn't a need."

"I'm pretty comfortable with them," Joe said. "Flower has started supplying virtual reality manuals with the Sharf two-man traders she's manufacturing. The visors give you the ability to walk through the circuits as if you were an electron with legs."

"Then maybe we should start your wife on the demo while the Verlocks are finishing up," the young man said. He quickly measured Kelly's pupillary distance with a simple ruler that had a slot cut lengthwise and a notch for the nose. Then he made a manual adjustment to a headset and helped the acting president get it to sit comfortably over her eyes and ears. She was just finishing the demonstration when her son walked in and snapped his fingers. Suddenly they were standing in the lobby of Human Empire headquarters.

"Hi, Mom," Samuel said. "Rose is sleeping in her stroller, but I'll ask Vivian to bring it out before we finish. You have the Verlock delegation with you?"

"Yes, but I think the emperor's grandson will be the only one to join us, unless they're improvising another headset for his tutor. I don't imagine the bodyguard would be very effective if he joined us in virtual reality."

"It depends on which virtual reality you're talking about. From what I've read about the history of these things, the original metaverse could be an ugly place."

There was a popping sound as Joe appeared in the virtual reality conference space, looked down for his missing legs, and laughed. "You should take advantage and ask me to dance, Kel. No stepping on your feet."

"Is the emperor's grandson joining us?"

"That's why I popped in. They ran into a last-minute technical snafu because the fiber optic cables weren't long enough. Whoever engineered these visors didn't believe in waste."

"So he's not coming?" Kelly asked.

"They cannibalized a second headset to extend the cables," Joe said. "A couple more minutes should do it."

"I heard that the ambassadors on Union Station are planning a site inspection of Earth for the new Historical Commission," Samuel said. "Any idea of what they're up to?"

"I'm not sure," his mother said. "You know how the aliens are. It might turn out that they wanted a free junket to Earth to visit the New World's Fair, or there could be some complication about the Alts originally being from here that they're trying to clean up. I heard from Dorothy that she's sending Richard to an Alt daycare now."

"We've had pretty good luck with our volunteer program to help the Alts that Flower transports to Earth Two acclimate to humans. The retirees enjoy participating, and the Alts find them less threatening than younger people."

"When you meet with the Alt leaders, do they ever talk about making Earth Two into an open world and inviting other aliens? Daniel brought up the possibility when he sat in for me on the EarthCent Intelligence Steering Committee holoconference last week."

"And you were there because you sat in for President Beyer," Samuel surmised. "Maybe we shouldn't talk too much about that because I'm not sure how secure virtual reality is. Are you with us, Flower?"

"I'm not going to tell anybody your secrets," the Dollnick AI responded.

"I meant, are these visor conferences secure since we're using the Stryxnet?"

"Unfortunately, you're also using virtual reality headsets manufactured on Earth a hundred years ago. The fiber optics are reasonably secure, but the processors are so noisy that a competent spy could eavesdrop from across the room, farther with appropriate antennas and amplification."

A vertical line appeared out of nowhere in front of the reception desk in the lobby, and then a pair of leathery hands reached through and peeled open reality. A Verlock stepped into the virtual meeting, looking like a well-drawn cartoon of the emperor's grandson, and he shuffled forward to meet Samuel.

"Emperor – McAllister?"

"First Administrator," Samuel said, even though he knew by this point that trying to correct the perceptions of aliens was a lost cause.

"Ernyad," the Verlock introduced himself. "My – grandfather – the – emperor – wished – for – me – to – express – his – regrets – that – his – schedule – prevented – him – from – making – the – trip – on – the – occasion – of – your – announcement."

All three of the McAllisters stared at Ernyad's avatar after this extraordinarily long speech. Finally, Kelly said, "I think there may be some mistake. The Human Empire has started on an accelerated path to replace EarthCent, but it has to pass a series of milestone reviews."

"We haven't even established a testing schedule yet," Samuel added.

"Details." The Verlock's avatar waved a hand dismissively and did a slow turn to survey the virtual reality representation of Human Empire headquarters on Flower. "You'll – need – more – space."

Fifteen

Dorothy slung her sewing bag over her shoulder, stuck a threaded needle in her sleeve for emergencies, and checked her inventory of virtual gold. "If you guys want to quit early and go to the tavern, it's on me," she told the others.

"Everybody fights, nobody quits," Dietro proclaimed. "We need to get into as much action as possible so Jyndal can strut her stuff."

"I don't know anything about combat magic," Baa's apprentice said nervously. "I only agreed to come because she says it's important for my development."

"It's important for her twenty-five percent of Dietro's cut if the show gets green-lighted," Dorothy said. "Have you made any progress with the Tharks, Ofer?"

"Their ambassador is traveling, but I know he'll be back for the next meeting of the Gambling Commission, so I'll ask him then. I just want to remind everybody that I'm a pacifist," Ofer added. "I'm only here to protect Jyndal."

"How are you going to protect her from a zombie or a skeleton warrior if you're not willing to fight?" Kevin asked.

"I'll try to get between them."

"Did you just say that the *Mage Search* show still hasn't been approved?" Tzachan asked. "If it's not a near certainty, then this isn't a business outing, and Flazint and I will have to count it as a date."

"It's a total certainty," Dietro told him. "The Grenouthians love the concept. The only thing we're missing is the contestants, and from what Ofer told us about how the Tharks protect their bookmaking operations by keeping tabs on anybody who regularly defies the odds, it's a sure thing that they'll be able to hook us up with talent."

"But what if they don't want to?" Flazint asked as she strung her bow. "The reason everybody uses the Tharks for questionable financial transactions is that they offer absolute confidentiality."

"To their clients," Affie told her Frunge friend. "If Ofer was right about the Tharks tracking sentients whose luck can't be explained by probability, it means that those individuals are a threat to the gambling industry. The Thark ambassador should be happy to expose them, and that might give Dietro leverage to get them to participate in the show."

"You're going to blackmail them?" Ofer asked. "I can't be a part of that."

"Nobody is going to blackmail anybody," Dietro said, shooting Affie an annoyed look. "Jyndal could tell you herself how frightening it was to manifest powers that she wasn't able to control. The show will help them see that they aren't alone in the galaxy and give them a chance to earn some honest money from their abilities."

"Maybe I could talk to them about forming a union."

"Is everybody ready?" Kevin asked. "The meter started running five minutes ago and LARPing studio time isn't cheap."

"It's going to be strange playing without Baa to bail us out," Dorothy said nervously. "Maybe we should stay away from dungeons and go to the town for market day instead. Doesn't the mayor always have quests to hand out for nice above-ground stuff?"

"We'll vote," Dietro said confidently. "Who wants to go on a boring quest to find a lost cow or dig an irrigation ditch?"

Dorothy, Ofer, and Jyndal raised their hands.

"The dungeons have it," the Vergallian said. "Let's go."

The party of eight adventurers entered the LARPing studio where they instantly found themselves in a desolate wasteland full of collapsed stone temples, the remains of houses, and in the distance, the breached and crumbling walls of the city.

"This is a new one," Kevin said. "I wonder what happened here?"

A floating bubble of light moved towards them, expanding as it came, and Ofer nervously stepped in front of his girlfriend.

"Don't worry," Affie told them. "It's an angel coming to tell us the history of this place. Something like this always happens for new games."

The bubble, now the size of a person, came to a halt in front of the group. A dazzling elf who radiated light from her very pores stepped onto the blackened ground.

"Welcome to the Realm of Ujaroon, Heroes. Here a battle for the very universe was fought, where the forces of light sacrificed themselves to lock the forces of darkness away for a thousand generations. But that time is rapidly coming to a close, and the Five Seals on the gates to the Demon Realms are beginning to crack. Will you undertake the task of eliminating the evil beings for once and for all?"

"By eliminate, do you mean kill?" Ofer asked before the others could accept the standard deal and find out what bonuses they would be granted. "Has anybody tried to negotiate with the demons, or is this one of those wars where nobody remembers why it started and they go on killing each other because that's what their fathers did?"

The elf, who had raised her arms to bestow a blessing, let them fall back to her sides. "The demons brought great evil to this realm," she said, clearly puzzled by the young scribe's attitude. "You can see the destruction they wrought."

"Did they, or did the alleged forces of light you talked about destroy their own city to prevent foreigners from immigrating?" Ofer demanded, becoming quite animated in his speech. "After all, we only have your word for what happened here. Maybe this was always a terrible, corrupt place, and the folks from the Demon Realm came here to bring enlightenment to the masses."

"Enough, Ofer," Jyndal said, tugging on his sleeve. "It's just a game."

"But it's the principle of the thing," he protested. "Just because she floated up in a bubble and is radiating light doesn't mean she's telling us the truth. Maybe it's a false flag operation."

"I seriously doubt that," Dietro said, but all the same he asked the elf, "Can you tell us who you are?"

"I am Aethelreda," she responded, drawing herself up indignantly. "I've never been so offended in my—what are you doing?" she demanded of Jyndal, who seemed to be tying an imaginary knot in the air.

"Casting identify," Baa's apprentice said apologetically. "It's one of the few spells I've gotten good at because I use it to test all of the rings I enchant to see if they're cursed."

"What level are you?" the elf asked in a voice that betrayed a sudden nervousness as her radiance seemed to flicker. "If you cast identify on a being too far above yourself, you could be injured by the blowback."

"Baa said you can never go wrong casting identify—it either works or it doesn't," Jyndal said as she tied off the knot. "There. Please identify your—"

"Now!" Aethelreda interrupted. Her radiance was suddenly extinguished, revealing a pit demon dressed in a loose robe of some sort. "I'll get the mage." She dashed forward to attack Jyndal, but Ofer managed to dive into her path. The two of them fell to the ground as an assorted group of monsters who had been concealed in shallow pits covered with loose dirt crawled out of their hiding places.

"Kevin, front line with me," Dietro shouted. "Tzachan and Flazint, pick your targets and fire at will. Affie, guard our mage."

"What about me?" Dorothy asked.

"Stay out of the way or go help Ofer. Maybe that demon witch is afraid of needles. I can't believe he was right."

Dorothy crouched low to stay out of the way of stray arrows, ran past where Affie had drawn a pair of daggers to protect Jyndal, and found Ofer had locked his arms and legs around the pit demon in a bear hug to prevent it from getting up.

"Let me go," the demon howled. "You're ruining my housecoat. Do you have any idea how hard it is to find something comfortable to wear that holds up to the fires of Hell?"

"Not until you promise to go away and leave us alone," Ofer grunted, his face turning red from the unaccustomed effort.

"I promise."

"Don't believe her," Dorothy said, dancing around the pair. "She already lied to us once."

"I can't hold her forever," Ofer said. "Take Jyndal and go back to the dressing room."

"Wait, I have an idea." Dorothy checked the progress of the fight and was relieved to see the low-level monsters falling back before the swords of her husband and Dietro. Then she knelt behind the demon and pulled the threaded needle from her sleeve. "Just try to keep her still for a minute."

"What are you doing?" the demon howled.

"I'm sewing the arms of your housecoat together so you can't cast any spells on us. Stop struggling or you might tear the fabric."

At this threat to its housecoat, the demon went limp, and Dorothy quickly secured its arms. Then she threaded another needle and took the slack out of the lower part of the coat down near the knees, so it fit almost as tightly over the demon's legs as a tube dress.

"All clear," Dietro called. "Anybody hurt?"

"Just blunt impact points, no bleeding," Kevin said. "What are you doing, Dorothy?"

"Finished," the seamstress said, rising to her feet. "You can let her up now."

Ofer let go of the demon, rolled over to put a little distance between them, and got shakily to his feet. "I don't understand," he said to the demon. "Why did you attack us? Jyndal wasn't going to hurt you."

"It was an ambush," Dietro told the young diplomat impatiently. "They were going to attack no matter what we did. If Jyndal hadn't identified the demon, it probably would have cursed us when we thought we were receiving a blessing, and then those low-level mobs might have done us in."

"Can somebody help me up?" the demon asked plaintively. "I can't move my arms, and it's going to be tough enough to balance on hooves with my knees practically touching."

"Do you promise not to attack us?" Ofer asked.

"Yes," the demon said, attempting to look remorseful. "I swear by the sacred fires of the Demon Realm."

"Somebody get her other arm," Ofer said. "She's surprisingly heavy for a holographic projection."

"That's the bot inside, and we don't talk about the mechanics of the LARPing studio while we're playing," Kevin said as he helped get the demon to its feet. "It's a good thing Jyndal cast that spell."

"But she never identified herself," Baa's apprentice said. "She interrupted me and attacked."

"Can you complete the casting now?" Flazint asked. "Maybe she's still hiding something."

Jyndal turned back to the demon and said, "Please identify yourself."

"Ballysthar, Pit Demon, Second Level," the monster reeled off.

"Does the identify spell let you ask it about the housecoat?" Dorothy asked the apprentice.

"I think I can extract aspects," Jyndal said. "Tell me about your housecoat."

"Rare housecoat, plus five to resistance from sacred fire and hellish flames," Ballysthar said sullenly. "I inherited it from my mom."

"Demons have mothers?" Ofer asked.

"Of course. Did you think we grew on trees?"

"But if you have mothers and clothes, how much difference can there be between us? Did you go to school?"

"Don't remind me," the demon said with a groan. "Have you ever heard of incorporeal punishment? One wrong answer and that wraith would make us hold our hands out and hit them with a ruler. I learned how to disguise myself as smarter students for protection, and then I just sort of fell into doing it after graduation."

"It's trying to gain our sympathy," Dietro said. "Don't listen to it."

"But what if Ballysthar is telling the truth?" Ofer objected. "This could be our chance to negotiate an equitable end to the violence for all parties."

Jyndal made a diamond shape with her thumbs and forefingers and peered through it at the pit demon. "I think she's telling the truth. At least, I don't see any evil intent."

"But she's a demon," Dietro said in frustration. "To her, evil intent might be classified as good. If you predict the actions of other species according to your own value system, you're likely to get your head handed to you on a pike."

"And you believe my species defines everything that I am?" the demon retorted. "You think that I've been waiting my whole life to travel to some alternative universe and ambush a party that looks like an advertisement for interspecies cooperation?"

"So what are you doing here?" Ofer asked. "Did you need the money?"

"Money? Do you think they pay us in the Demon Realms for traveling here and putting our lives on the line? Why do you think I was so worried about my housecoat? They won't even reimburse us for expenses or damages to our kit."

"She's just trying to gain our sympathy," Dietro repeated, but he could tell that the others were weakening. "Look, Ballysthar. We're willing to give you a break, but you have to meet us halfway. Show us how to get through the dungeon and we'll let you go."

"I can't do that," the demon said. "They'll kill me. Not just once, but over and over again until they get bored."

"Until who gets bored," Ofer asked.

"The devils. They're the ones you should be talking to. I can take you to them if you want."

"It's a trap," Dietro said. "Can't you tell that she's been trained to tell us all of this in case she fell into enemy hands? It's too pat, too well-rehearsed."

"Are you lying to us?" Jyndal asked sternly, peering at the prisoner through the diamond formed by her fingers and thumbs.

"I swear on my mother's pyre," Ballysthar said. "Just give me a chance to prove myself."

"We'll make a contract," Tzachan said. "Ofer, you're a scribe. Do you have any writing supplies?"

"I have three sheets of parchment, a bottle of ink, and one fine quill," the young man said after double-checking his pouch.

"All right. Can you take dictation?"

"Let me find something to write on." Ofer spotted a flat stone slab in the broken temple nearby and led the party over. "This will do fine."

"It looks like an altar," Affie said. "Check for bloodstains."

"Nothing, it's clean."

"You can't go by that," the demon said, obviously uncomfortable within the boundaries of the former temple.

"It rains here constantly. You just happened to show up during one of the breaks."

"Take this down," Tzachan said. "I, Ballysthar, do solemnly swear on the pyre of my mother, that I shall do no harm to the members of the SBJ Fashions party, consisting of Flazint, Dorothy, Affie, Jyndal, Kevin, Ofer, Dietro, and Tzachan, nor shall I, through inaction, allow them to come to harm. I pledge to arrange a meeting between said party and a devil of the Demon Realms in a place and time that will maximize the safety of said party. I further pledge not to contact any other inhabitants of the Demon Realm to inform them of my situation unless such action is required to arrange the meeting with a devil. Signed, Ballysthar, Pit Demon."

Ofer finished writing a fraction of a second after the Frunge attorney stopped dictating and extended the quill to the demon.

Ballysthar didn't move. "Do you expect me to hold it in my mouth?" she asked.

"Oh, right," Dorothy said. "But if I cut your arms loose, you have to promise—"

"Not to injure, curse, frighten, or through my inaction allow any others to rain on your parade," the demon interrupted impatiently. "This is embarrassing enough as is, and I prefer to get it over with as soon as possible."

Dorothy took out her favorite sewing scissors and expertly cut through the stitches holding the housecoat's sleeves together, and by extension, the demon's arms.

"Right," Ballysthar said and accepted the quill. "I'll just give this a quick read and—what are you trying to pull here?"

"What do you mean?" Tzachan asked.

"I have the translate languages skill, it's part of my forked-tongue package, but this is just gibberish."

"Let me see it," Affie said, slipping closer to the altar. "That's not any version of Humanese that I know."

"It's legal shorthand," Ofer explained. "I took a course from my teacher bot growing up because I thought I might return to Earth and become a court reporter."

The demon folded her arms across her chest. "I'm not signing that. My mother didn't raise any fools."

"Can you write it out longhand, Ofer?" Tzachan asked. "You said you have three sheets of parchment."

"I don't think I have enough ink," the scribe said.

"Look," Ballysthar said. "You trust me, or you don't. At the end of the day, I'll be back in my universe, and all of you NPCs will return to wherever the artificial intelligence keeps you when we're not playing."

"What are you talking about?" Dietro demanded. "We're all real. You're the non-player character."

"What's going on? Did I accidentally pick a retro gaming chamber? Faking sentience through contradiction is the crudest thing I've ever seen."

"I'm not contradicting—listen," Dietro said earnestly. "The eight of us are all here on a Stryx station in a LARPing studio, but we grew up in different locations all around the galaxy—"

"Except me," Dorothy interjected. "I was born on Union Station."

"Next you're going to try to convince me that you're real because your history stretches back millions of years and there are trillions of you," Ballysthar said in a bored voice. "Do you think I don't have a backstory? Do you think my cowardly friends—" she glanced around the desolate scene of destruction and failed to spot any of her support team from the ambush, "—don't have backstories? We all went to school together, and they're still mad that I used to disguise myself as them to get out of trouble. If you want to meet a devil, come with me and I'll lead you out of this dungeon to a portal that will take us to the real universe."

"I can't accept that reality would be called the Demon Realms," Ofer said. "The rest of your story might be true, but if we're all NPCs in some simulation you're playing, why would you refer to yourselves as demons and devils?"

For a second, the SBJ Fashions party thought that the demon was pointing at her ear, but then they realized she was extracting a small bullet-shaped device. "Try this," she said. "I don't know what you're using for translation technology, but I won't understand you while this is out."

Ofer accepted the translation device, held it close to his ear without inserting it into the canal, and said, "Somebody say something."

"Demon," Kevin said.

The scribe paled and handed the bullet-shaped translator back to Ballysthar.

"What did you hear?" Dorothy demanded.

"Human," Ofer whispered.

"Why does this happen every time we go LARPing together?" Dietro complained. "Okay, fine. We're all NPCs produced by your game or whatever to entertain you, Ballysthar. Take us to your devil, who I have no doubt is really an angel, and we'll tell you where we keep our pot of gold."

"Gold would be good," Ballysthar said and looked hopefully at Dorothy. "Would you mind?"

Dorothy crouched and snipped the stitches she'd used to gather the housecoat around the demon's knees, and then they all followed Ballysthar to what might have been the entrance of an empty mine.

"How far is it," Tzachan asked. "Real or not, we're paying for our time in here."

"There's a shortcut through the mirror," Ballysthar said. "It's a narrow passage, so we'll have to go single file."

"You go first," Dietro ordered when the demon pointed to a mirror the size of a door. "No tricks."

"No tricks."

Everybody expected the mirror to be hinged like a door, but Ballysthar stepped directly into it with a rippling effect like a pebble thrown into a pool of water. The reflection dissipated once she was inside the passage and turned around, and suddenly a barred grate rose out of the floor, barring the path through the mirror. The demon began to laugh.

"What are you doing?" Ofer demanded. "You gave us your word."

"I didn't sign anything, sucker, and for your information, my forked tongue skill works perfectly well on legal shorthand."

"It's a trap!" Dietro said. "Let's get out of here."

Another grate sprang out of the floor sealing off the entrance of the mine shaft, and more monsters crowded into the passage behind Ballysthar, laughing and hurling insults.

"Do something," Dorothy urged Kevin. "I don't want to get killed by demons."

"I can't believe I was so wrong," Ofer said. "I'm sorry Jyndal. I failed to protect you."

"Don't worry," Jyndal said. "Baa told me that something like this can always happen, so she gave me a scroll to read."

"What does it do?"

"Group teleport," she said, drawing it out of her sleeve and unrolling it.

"Cowards," Ballysthar howled as the eight players disintegrated in sparkles of light.

Sixteen

Judith carefully placed her baby in the carrier on her display desk and then waited to see if the lack of motion would end the new sleep cycle. The door to Ofer's office slid open and she spun on him with a cautionary finger to her lips. The consul turned meekly and tiptoed back into his office. A minute later, she followed him.

"Sorry," she said to the young diplomat, and remained standing at the door so she could keep an eye and an ear on her baby. "It was a long night, probably something I ate."

"Something you ate?" Ofer asked in surprise. "Don't you mean something the baby ate?"

"You have noticed that I'm nursing, haven't you?" Judith asked him. "You know, mammals? What the mother eats the baby drinks?"

"I forgot." He hesitated for a moment, and then said, "I started working on my history of EarthCent again to surprise Kelly when she gets back, but I'm hung up on the training camp for intelligence agents. According to my notes, the ambassador's husband told me that they started it in Mac's Bones because he had the space, and he recruited his former commanding officer from the mercenaries to run it."

"Pyun Woojin, I used to work for him. Then he got tapped to become Flower's captain, though from what he says, his main duties are performing marriages and staying out of the way."

"And then Thomas," Ofer glanced at his notes, "the artificial person who was EarthCent Intelligence's first agent, took over the training camp, with you and Joe helping."

"And Chance," Judith added. "She's an artificial person too. She and Thomas live together, but I don't know if they ever officially tied the knot."

"But the part that confuses me is when they started training Galactic Free Press reporters. Is your husband also a spy?"

"Bob? If he is, he hasn't told me about it. Journalists and spies don't train together. The course for reporters was started after a few of them got kidnapped by pirates while on assignment. The paper pays for kidnap avoidance training because it's cheaper than ransom. And they get the basic alien etiquette training at the same time."

"Like how to greet royalty and which fork to use on the melon?" Ofer asked.

"EarthCent Intelligence hires unemployed alien actors to role-play different situations with the trainees," Judith explained. "The focus is on not causing problems out of ignorance of cultural norms, and if need be, de-escalating misunderstandings."

"Do you think they would let me observe?"

"You can take the training if you want," Judith said. "Shaina and Brinda have the cookbook under control, and Daniel is next door if anything important comes up. I asked Donna if the embassy was always so slow when she was working here, and she said that the aliens all know that Kelly will be back, so they're just waiting on most issues. A few months doesn't mean much to species that live ten times as long as we do."

"I didn't realize that," Ofer said. "Maybe I should take the training."

"I'll ping Thomas and find out when the next available slot opens. Was there anything else?"

"Daniel and I are going to the Gambling Commission meeting at the off-world betting parlor, and I don't think I'll be back today. The last time the Thark ambassador got us all into a card game."

"How badly did you lose?" Judith asked out of curiosity.

"Just the forced antes," Ofer said. "I never bet."

The embassy manager shook her head in mock despair and retreated to her display desk. The consul made a quick note of what he had learned, the time, and the source, and then said, "Libby?"

"Jyndal is resting."

"How did you know I was going to ask about Jyndal?"

"You aren't exactly a cipher, Consul. Shall I ping Daniel that you're coming to meet him?"

"Yes, thank you." Ofer started to get up, and then he repeated, "Libby?"

"Now I'd just be guessing," the Stryx station librarian responded.

"Can you contact Stats?"

"It depends on your purpose. If you want to tell the artificial intelligence who raised you that you're doing well and are among your own kind, I can do that, but it wouldn't be fair to the other tunnel network members to pass along any information that could impact their future business dealings. It's complicated by the fact that you're now a diplomat."

"I understand. Just a message to say that I'm doing well and that I hope to see him again sometime to thank him for everything now that I'm happy to be alive. Oh, and that some of our ideas about political economy work better in theory than in practice."

"I'll pass along the message," Libby said.

Ofer left the embassy and walked down two doors to avoid the shared conference room where he knew Shaina and Brinda were holding another meeting related to the *All Species Cookbook*. The latest in a long line of receptionists in CoSHC's shared workplace failed to recognize Ofer and asked him to wait, then notified Daniel of the visitor using the intercom system.

"It's the off-world betting parlor today, right?" Daniel asked when he came out of his office. "Remind me to check the odds on the Human Empire milestones."

"I still don't understand why the Stryx allow everyone to gamble on the future of humanity," Ofer said. "Won't it result in some aliens rooting against us, and if they've wagered large amounts, they would have a motivation to see us fail."

"I don't think the milestones are something that can be affected by a few unhappy punters, and you're not giving the Tharks enough credit. Anybody placing large bets and then trying to influence the outcome is going to draw their scrutiny, and nobody wants that. The Tharks almost destroyed themselves through internecine conflicts over clan honor before the survivors settled into a role as the interspecies bankers and bookmakers of last resort."

"I didn't know that. Are there any good histories I can read?"

"Happened millions of years ago," Daniel said. They entered the lift tube, and he gave their destination. "You might get the same basics I just told you from the station librarian, but outside of academia, the advanced species consider each other's history private business, and it's not something the Tharks like to talk about. I suspect the Verlocks or the Grenouthians could give you a better idea of what went on, but they'd probably refuse out of respect for the Tharks."

"What's the point of having a Historical Commission if some species aren't even willing to share their history?" Ofer demanded. "I was under the impression that half of the entertainment industry was based on reenactments or prying into each other's past. The Grenouthians certainly make enough documentaries about Earth, and they don't pull any punches about all of our mistakes."

"Human history is all so recent that the aliens don't take it seriously," Daniel said. "I wouldn't be surprised if they have a different word for it. And I think somebody told me that Thark history is largely taboo even among Tharks. Maybe the only way they broke the cycle of violence was to stop keeping track of whose father killed whose brother and put it all behind them."

"But you're talking about willful ignorance."

"Some problems can't be fixed, Ofer. You're still adjusting to the sloppy realities of living with biologicals after being brought up by artificial intelligence, but we all seem to go through self-destructive phases, which is why there are so many Galactic Heritage Sites commemorating lost civilizations that were far more advanced than anything on Earth. I know that some of the other ambassadors believe that the Stryx set up the tunnel network as an experiment to see if they could preserve more species in the long run."

"Then why not intervene before those civilizations develop interstellar travel like they did for Earth?" Ofer asked as they exited the lift tube. "Joe told me that the most dangerous phase for any sentient species is when they master their environment with technology before they develop the ability to move elsewhere if something goes wrong."

"Maybe the Stryx have come to the same conclusion and Earth is a new experiment, but they don't want to micromanage the whole galaxy," Daniel said, waving as he spotted the Drazen ambassador on his way to the row of betting windows. "I wonder if he's got a hot tip. Why don't you find where everybody is sitting, and I'll catch up?"

Ofer bit back a comment about the propriety of gambling at a meeting of the Gambling Commission, in part because he had no idea what was considered acceptable behavior. For some reason, access to the main floor was restricted that day by a coin-operated turnstile that activated a sort of slot machine that was paying off in tokens. He followed Daniel through, paying with a one-cred coin, and was rewarded with a half-cred's worth of tokens in return.

He spotted the Thark Ambassador sitting alone at a collection of tables that had been pushed together near the corner of the big board displaying race results from all over the galaxy. The alien seemed to have a sixth sense for when somebody was looking at him, because he turned to face the consul, who made his way over.

"Interested in a sure thing?" the Thark ambassador asked before Ofer could sit. "All of the others are in on it."

"I'm not really a gambler," Ofer said, but he hesitated over sitting. "All of them?"

"It's a classic case of mispricing. Sometimes members of a species let pride in their identity overcome common sense, and they back a native long shot over the odds-on favorite, making for attractive investment odds."

"How much will the ambassadors wager?"

"A few creds, no more than five. Just enough so they don't feel embarrassed in front of the betting window tellers."

"Then I don't understand. How much could they possibly make betting that little on a favorite?"

"Less than a cred," the Thark ambassador said. "It's not about the money, it's about being on the right side of the bet. Everybody likes making the smart play."

"But they didn't figure it out themselves. You tipped them."

The little alien shrugged. "There's give and take in everything we do, and I'm the host. I trust them not to put down a million creds and make things awkward for me."

Ofer sat down, and then moved his chair closer to the ambassador and lowered his voice. "Would it be okay if I brought up a private business matter?"

"Of course," the Thark said. "Business makes the tunnel network go 'round."

"My girlfriend works for SBJ Fashions as, well, a sorcerer's apprentice under Baa, and the sales manager—"

"Dietro," the ambassador interjected. "He's on the list."

"The list? No, never mind that for now," Ofer amended himself. "Dietro has been working on a reality show about a magical talent search for the Grenouthian network for the last year, but they're having a problem finding contestants. I remembered what you said about banning gamblers who are beyond lucky, and it occurred to me that they might be, uh, magical."

"Go on."

"Well, I thought that if you ban cheaters who aren't using technology, you must keep track of them somehow so you can tell if they're placing bets through proxies, or doing whatever they do to otherwise influence the outcomes of gambling propositions."

"Without confirming or denying your supposition, I can say that it's logical."

Ofer realized that the Thark ambassador was waiting for a concrete proposal. "So maybe you could contact the aliens on your blacklist and tell them the show will allow them to make some money and meet other, well, magic wielders."

"And?"

"I offered to talk to you for him since I've been coming to your meetings and you're nice to me," Ofer said. "Dietro warned me not to negotiate a deal because I don't have any experience, but he said the Grenouthian network would be willing to discuss either a head fee or an interest in the production if you can help."

"That's what I was waiting to hear," The Thark ambassador said, rubbing his hands together. "There's no question that some of the individuals on our watch list could be regarded as magical, at least for the purposes of a talent search show. Some of them use their innate ability without being aware of it and may welcome the chance to get answers about themselves. I'll contact Dietro after the meeting and see if we can come to a mutually agreeable arrangement."

"What are you two whispering about?" Czeros asked, taking his seat on the other side of the Thark. "Saving your best tips for your Human protégé?"

"Me?" Ofer asked in surprise. "I don't know anything about gambling."

"I beg to differ," the Thark ambassador said. "Bookmaking is nothing more than applied history. Did you think we make odds on a horse race by asking the quadrupeds how they feel about their chances?"

"History without statistical analysis is just so much old gossip," Srythlan said ponderously as he lowered his bulk into a chair across the table from the Thark ambassador. "Given enough data, a Verlock historian can not only provide a definitive explanation for why events unfolded the way they did but tell you what would have happened if different paths had been chosen."

"I think I forgot my betting slip at the window," Czeros said, shooting Ofer a wink and starting back in the direction from which the other ambassadors were arriving. He exchanged a few brief words with them and pointed at Srythlan, then the whole group did an about-face and headed for the snack bar.

"But what's the difference between that and the fiction books Ambassador McAllister kept pushing on me?" Ofer asked the Verlock. "There's no way you can prove the accuracy of your alternative histories when the events never took place."

"Statistics don't lie, my young friend," Srythlan boomed. "The methodology employed by our historians is amenable to proofs, and controlled experiments have shown the accuracy of the error bars bracketing the range of outcomes."

"So you're saying it's not a single prediction, but a series of possibilities with probabilities assigned."

"Near certainties. For example, I recently read an alternative history of what would have happened on Earth if the Stryx hadn't stepped in to save your planet from suicidal monetary policies. The most important thing in your twenty-first century was money, yet your central banks did their best to undermine the foundations of the international system of exchange for temporary and illusory gains."

"Could I get a copy of that?" Ofer asked. "I'd love to know what might have happened."

"Not might have happened—would have happened," the Verlock ambassador insisted. "How old are you?"

"Twenty-six, I think."

"You're too young. Come back and ask me again when you're forty."

"How can I be too young to read an alternative history of my own people? I started on the real history before I was ten, and it was pretty awful."

"Was this 'real history' you refer to accompanied by mathematical proofs?" Srythlan inquired.

"No, but it was on my teacher bot," Ofer said.

"Feh! Teacher bots pass on the accepted knowledge of your species. That doesn't mean that it's right."

"Couldn't I get an edited version then?"

"It's too horrible," the Verlock said. "Just thinking about it ruins my appetite for the salty chips I think I see my Grenouthian colleague purchasing at the snack bar."

"At least give him a hint," the Thark ambassador said. "Fourteen years is a long time for a human to wait."

"Everybody dies. There was one man left in the end, I believe his name was Smith, and he dragged himself to the ocean in hopes that his decaying body would spawn a new cycle of life, at least on the microscopic level. It didn't."

"I'm sorry, but there's no way that a statistical analysis of history could produce the name of the last remaining survivor and detail his death like that," Ofer said, folding his arms across his chest. "I know I'm nowhere near the level of a Verlock mathematician, but what you're describing sounds more like one of those apocalyptic dramas everybody gets excited about."

Srythlan looked puzzled for a moment, and then he said, "You're right, I got them confused. It's funny how immersive productions can make a greater impression on our memories than scientifically accurate treatises. But that doesn't change the fact that it would have gone poorly with your species if the Stryx hadn't intervened."

"Help yourself, Ofer." Daniel set a takeout tray with two coffees and two corn muffins on the table between himself and the consul. "Ortha is bringing your usual, Ambassador," he said to the Thark. "Do you need me to move some chairs around to make room for members of the public? I saw in your scheduling note that you published a special invitation to residents of Union Station who wish to express their disapproval of gambling."

"I don't think they'll be much bother," the Thark ambassador said. "Didn't you enter through the turnstile?"

"We didn't have a choice, but I spent the tokens at the snack bar, so it made no difference."

"Technically, putting a coin in a turnstile and receiving an undefined quantity of tokens in return is gambling."

"That should keep them out," the Grenouthian ambassador said, setting another takeout tray on the table. "Crute pinged and asked me to apologize that he'll be late, but he's at the Chert embassy discussing renovations."

"There are enough of us to get started, and I wasn't planning any votes today," the Thark ambassador said. "Where's Ortha with my drink?"

"He saw a proposition on the big board that he couldn't resist and went back to the windows to place a bet," Bork said, taking the seat on Daniel's left. "Why don't we get the

Human Empire issue out of the way first since the Hortens are indifferent."

"The Hortens don't care what happens to us?" Ofer asked.

"They're the only species on the tunnel network that has no tradition of lotteries. The lack of strategy rubs their gaming instincts the wrong way."

"The best strategy is not to buy a ticket, since it has no statistical impact on your chance of winning," the Thark ambassador said with a chuckle. "You have a better chance of getting hit by a meteor than picking the winning combination in a multi-planet lottery."

"I always do the quick pick," Bork said.

"And have you won?"

The Drazen ambassador mumbled something about hitting for a free ticket once.

"Right. This meeting is called to order and all of that, and we'll start with the lottery issue. Daniel, if the Human Empire wants to go ahead with a lottery, they'll either have to negotiate separate deals with every local government where chances are sold or come up with a technological method to restrict ticket sales to Humans."

"Samuel was talking about offering it as an add-on to the GenePost app, which is restricted to humans by default."

The Thark ambassador chuckled. "I should have known. GenePost was the idea of Blythe's daughter, and I've never known a Human with a better head for business. I bet that Vivian was planning the lottery angle from the start. A gambling platform that uses pre-registration through DNA samples to confirm the species. What will the kids think of next?"

Seventeen

"She's already been in there for ten minutes," EarthCent's acting president said to her special assistant. "Do you think I should go check on her?"

Aabina was so startled by this proposal that she stepped in front of Kelly to block the path to the all-species bathroom. "Ten minutes is usual for a young Sharf," she said in a whisper. "The emperor's great-granddaughter may not have even started yet depending on the last species to use the facility. The conversion from a Huktra or Tyrellian commode back to a more standard humanoid configuration takes several minutes."

"I seem to remember from somewhere that the Sharf have a whole ritual that involves washing up afterward," Joe added.

"But they don't talk about that in public, especially around aliens," Aabina responded, still in a whisper. "Why don't the two of you take a quick rest at the open-air café over there and I'll wait for her to come out."

"I get the feeling we've been demoted," Kelly said to her husband with a laugh. "Well, I wouldn't mind getting off my feet for a few minutes. Yvella has been running us ragged."

"I guess we'll take you up on that, Aabina," Joe said. "Can I bring you back anything?"

"I have a water bottle in my bag if I get thirsty," the Vergallian said. "I'm enjoying the sun."

Kelly and Joe made their way through the crowd of fairgoers to the collection of tables that were equipped with large beach umbrellas, and on spotting a waitress, took seats at an empty table rather than approaching the counter. Kelly brought out her smartphone, which in over four months on Earth had become almost an extension of her arm, and checked for messages.

"Look, Joe," she said, turning the screen so he could read it. "It's from Bella. The Historical Commission on Union Station has received final approval for their site visit. All of our friends will be coming to Earth next month."

"I'm glad we don't pay taxes because I'd hate to think that this is what they were being spent on," Joe said. "An all-expenses-paid vacation to Earth that just happens to coincide with the New World's Fair and your temporary term as EarthCent's president? There must be a special word for this kind of thing, but it's not coming to mind."

"Boondoggle," Kelly said. "But I'm not sure it applies in this case. From what Daniel told me on our last tunneling conference call, the commission doesn't even have a choice in the matter. The Stryx procedure for potential historical designations is that all of the ambassadors who can breathe the atmosphere of the candidate world have to participate in the decision and make the site visit. He said that the other ambassadors have been reading up on Earth's ancient history, though for some of them, I'm sure that means they've been watching Grenouthian documentaries."

"And the point of all of this is to grant recognition of Neanderthal archeological finds as Alt heritage sites?" Joe asked as he gave the waitress a little wave to indicate they were ready to order.

"Daniel was pretty vague about that part, and I'm not surprised. I've sat on plenty of committees over the years, but only one commission, and I never really figured out what we were doing there. In addition to filling in for me on my regular committees, Daniel has been stuck on two new commissions, though he's let Ofer attend a few Gambling Commission meetings in his place."

"Any fresh juice you have for me, doesn't matter what," Joe told the waitress when she arrived. "Kelly?"

"Juice sounds good. And in to-go cups, please, because we're waiting for friends."

"We've got orange juice in single-serving bottles," the girl said, but when she looked over to Kelly for confirmation, something clicked, and she became excited. "I know you. You're that, uh—"

"Acting President of EarthCent, but it's really no big deal," Kelly said.

"No, not that. You play, uh, the grandmother in that immersive about the lost colony ship. What's it called again?"

"I'm afraid that's somebody else," Joe told the girl. "We've been married for over thirty years and Kelly has been an EarthCent diplomat the whole time."

"Oh," the waitress said in disappointment. "You look a lot like what's-her-name, but maybe it's just the skirt suit. I'll bring your juice."

"That was different," Kelly said with a wry smile after the girl left. "I finally get recognized on Earth and it's as the wrong person. I'll have to tell Dorothy that her skirt suit design is being worn by a famous actress."

"I can't get over how little attention we've drawn taking the delegations around the fair," Joe said. "Fifty years ago, all the kids would come running if they saw aliens on Earth. Nowadays, it takes wings or a long tail to attract attention, maybe both."

"Keep in mind that we're just a monorail ride away from the city. Things may be different in less populated areas of the world."

"Maybe, but if everybody is watching the Grenouthian news and Vergallian dramas on their phones and playing in Horten gaming tournaments, I wouldn't be too sure." He glanced back towards the all-species restrooms where Aabina was patiently waiting for the Sharf emperor's great-granddaughter to emerge. "Funny that Yvella traveled alone without any escort. Do you think that means that the Sharf don't take us seriously?"

"It may mean that they're taking EarthCent's integration into the Human Empire for granted, and they don't see the point of wasting resources on a state visit to a caretaker government, especially since EarthCent's authority on Earth was always highly limited," Kelly said. Her expression changed as if she'd just remembered something important, and she began tapping out a note to herself on the smartphone with her thumbs. "That's exactly what's been bugging me. Thank you, Joe."

"It's always sad when an old pencil-and-paper person switches to screens. Have you put away your paperback notebooks for good?"

"What? Oh, I didn't even notice," Kelly said, putting down her phone and fishing her notebook out of her purse.

"What's been bugging you?" Joe asked when he realized he'd interrupted her usual process, in which she told him what she was thinking while writing herself a note so she wouldn't forget.

"What's been missing from all of these goodwill tours we've been giving the visiting diplomatic delegations. Nobody has tried to make any deals or asked for any favors for second cousins or third nephews twice removed. They look at the exhibits, make polite comments, do a virtual reality meeting with Samuel when we get to the Human Empire pavilion, and thank us for taking them around."

"I suppose you're right, but we've done at least four times as many tours for visiting business delegations, and they haven't been shy about asking for extraterritorial status and whatever other perks EarthCent can grant them."

"They're businessmen, you expect that," Kelly said, looking back and forth between the counter and where they had left Aabina, and rising to her feet. "Yvella just came out, Joe, and I can't make her wait. Can you pay for the juice and then catch up with us?"

"Where will you be?"

"I'm not sure, but I'll enable that beacon app that Larry showed us, and you can just home in with your phone." She was swiping and tapping even as she spoke, and then she showed Joe the screen with its stylized representation of a ping radiating waves in a circle. "All set."

"Okay. I'll call if it doesn't work," Joe said.

Kelly met Aabina and Yvella at the midpoint between the restrooms and the café. "My husband is taking a quick break and he'll catch up with us," she told her guest. "Is there anything special you wanted to see before we head for the Human Empire pavilion?"

"I'm just a student," the skeletal young Sharf said in embarrassment. "This is my first diplomatic mission ever. My parents were supposed to do it, but they're waiting at Onkle Four for the grand opening."

"That's perfectly fine," Kelly said with a laugh, wondering what grand opening the girl was talking about, but not wanting to ask for fear that it would sound like she was questioning Sharf priorities. "Yours is the last diplomatic mission I'm expecting from any of the species we have relations with, and none of the delegations were here to open negotiations or anything like that."

"Thank you. They told me you have a reputation for keeping everything casual. I'm just hoping to learn more about humanity while I'm here. Whatever knowledge I have of your species is academic, anything you want to show me would be equally useful."

"Then perhaps we'll try some of the cultural performances. Just let me check the information channel and see what there is within walking distance that's about to start."

While Kelly was staring off into space and reading on her heads-up display, something cold was pressed into her hand, and she heard Joe say, "I loosened the cap so you can get it off, but it's tight enough not to drip."

"Can you deactivate my location ping?" she asked without turning her head. "Larry said it runs down the battery."

She felt a slight tug on her shoulder as Joe went into her purse to dig out the phone and close the app. Then she spotted a light-yellow bar over a performance that a member of the Dollnick delegation had told her was certainly unique to Earth. As she closed her heads-up display, Aabina was just explaining to the Sharf girl that the carved ponies on the nearby carousel were limited to going up and down and in circles and couldn't be rented for independent rides.

"How strange," Yvella said. "It looks so much like a mechanical Frolk display from my world that I was sure you had copied the idea from us. It's funny how cultures can independently develop such similar ideas, even if they ultimately serve a different purpose."

"So true," Kelly said. "We're just a short walk away from the Roman pavilion, which celebrates thousands of years of developments from one of the cradles of civilization on our world. If we're in time, we'll see a demonstration that utilizes tiles that may have been invented by the Chinese civilization a thousand years earlier."

When they arrived at the Italian pavilion, a large crowd had already gathered in the garden area outside to see the demonstration, which was only held once a day. The ground had been landscaped with a gentle slope to form a sort of natural amphitheater for evening opera performances, so even though they had arrived late, Kelly and her party had a decent view of the proceedings.

"What are they doing?" Yvella asked, straining her eye stalks to take in the strange scene. "It looks like a sort of giant mosaic, except all of the tiles are black, and some of them seem to be sticking up too far."

A little girl had been chosen from the crowd to participate, and trembling with anticipation, she reached out and gently pushed over the black tile that the exhibition manager indicated.

Dominoes began to fall, quickly branching out into tributaries that created a scene of a galley at sea. The timing was so exquisite that all the oars seemed to move at the same time, thrusting the prow forward as an improbable black wave crashed over the deck. The artists who had built the moving picture were purists, so all the dominos used were black tiles with white dots, but ultimately, it gave the display a certain gravitas, like an ink drawing.

"That was worshipful," the Sharf said breathlessly when the last domino fell. "Can you ask them to do it again?"

"Not until tomorrow morning," Joe told her. "I've stopped by early to see them setting up. There's a whole team of youngsters who arrive at midnight after the opera is finished and work straight through until go-time."

"Do you mean that Humans set those tiles up one at a time? It wasn't done by a robot?"

"Nothing artificial about it. The only difference between what you saw toppling over and what I've seen during setup is that they use spacers, like firebreaks, so if somebody accidentally knocks over a domino, they don't lose all of their work."

"Do the Sharf have dominoes?" Kelly asked.

"Yes," Yvella replied. "We don't have little dots on ours, just two colors. I haven't seen toppling before, so either we never came up with it, or it went out of style."

"That happens a lot," Aabina said. "I'd never seen domino toppling either, but I sent a question to the Vergallian Imperial Library after witnessing the demonstration, and a researcher replied that it's one of those things that comes around in cycles. There have been outdoor tile races on Vergallian worlds where tens of millions of our version of dominos have been knocked over."

"Do you have any other demonstrations like this?" the Sharf emperor's great-granddaughter asked Kelly, who was in the act of taking a swig from her bottle of orange juice.

"Do you mean strictly toppling demonstrations, or would anything involving balancing or mechanical complexity do?" Joe asked.

"Balance and mechanical complexity are both important. One of our most popular art forms, dating back to the first de-automation movement, features machines that employ a large number of moving parts to accomplish a task that could be done by hand with much less effort."

"Rube Goldberg machines. There's a large one set up by the Old Way movement that's intended as a commentary on our addiction to automation. Do we have time to swing by on the way to the Human Empire pavilion, Kel?"

EarthCent's acting president checked her Dollnick wristwatch. "The conference isn't scheduled for another forty-five minutes. Have you ever used a virtual reality visor, Yvella?"

"I'm not sure I know what one is," the Sharf girl said. "My translation implies a sort of hat that fools my brain into thinking I'm elsewhere."

"It's less of a hat than a bulky pair of eyeglasses that—" Kelly broke off as the Sharf's eyestalks swiveled in her direction. "I know you can retract your eyeballs into the sockets, but can you keep them there? The visor will fit over the upper part of your face and cover your eyes, and you wouldn't want them popping out and hitting the screens."

"My reflexes would prevent that from ever happening."

"Like upper caste Vergallians would never release pheromones while sleeping," Aabina commented.

Joe led the way along a route that he was obviously familiar with, and five minutes later they arrived near an enormously complicated machine that had been built on a raised platform so people could see most of the action even if they weren't close. Several steel balls were in motion at the same time, dropping through baffles, running through mazes, rolling through tubes, and exiting by jumping between the vanes of windmills turned by gears powered by other falling balls.

"It's magnificent, but what does it do?" Yvella asked after watching with rapt attention for several minutes.

"Do you see the cage with the chicken? Its feeder dispenses a pellet of chicken feed whenever one of the steel balls—here comes one now," Joe said, pointing as a ball reached the end of a screw-driven elevator and rolled into the bowl of a large wooden spoon. A light chain attached to the handle of the spoon pulled up a lever on the pellet dispenser as the weight of the ball caused the bowl of the spoon to drop and dump it into the top of a hopper full of steel balls.

"It reminds me of the perpetual motion machines we were always trying to build in nursery school before we learned about the conservation of energy," the Sharf girl said. "Thank you for showing it to me."

Aabina led the way back to the Human Empire pavilion where they all donned the virtual reality headsets that had somehow become the featured part of every diplomatic tour. Kelly was used to the visors by this point and almost preferred them over holoconferences, which had always seemed uncomfortably real. The avatars helped her remember that the attendees might be separated by interstellar distances, which helped cut down on the number of times that she told somebody to just stop by her office to pick something up.

Samuel's avatar had a mischievous look on its face when they ported in, but he would only say that there was a surprise waiting in the conference room. He led them through the virtual lobby of Human Empire headquarters to a closed door and invited Yvella to step through first.

"Mom! Dad! What are you doing on Flower?" the Sharf girl demanded.

"We aren't on Flower," her father informed her, his eye stalks waggling just like a cartoon character's. "The grand opening was a success, and Onkle Four now has access to the Stryx tunnel network and all that implies. Emperor McAllister asked our representative on Flower to send us virtual reality headsets in preparation for this day, and they arrived just in time."

"What did I miss?" Kelly asked, reflexively turning to her husband's avatar even though he had been with her the whole time.

"Onkle Four is an open world near the center of the Sharf Empire, in their old industrial cluster," Samuel jumped in to explain. "They've reached twenty million human inhabitants, so the Stryx connected them to the tunnel network."

"I feel like you're in the room with me," Yvella said to her parents. "You have to come to the New World's Fair. They have artists who spend all night setting up tens of thousands of little tiles just so they can knock them all down, and a do-nothing machine that does even less with more motion than the one in the spaceport at home."

"We plan to make Earth our first destination, since we owe the Humans and their nascent empire for getting us access to the tunnel network without having to sign the treaty," her father said. "Cancel your return ticket and we'll come and pick you up in the imperial yacht. Do you think you can keep busy on Earth for another two weeks on their calendar?"

"Oh, yes. I could spend the whole time at the fair."

"Was Onkle Four the only Sharf open world attempting to build a human population of twenty million to get a tunnel network connection?" Kelly asked. "Ever since we first noticed that option in the updated treaty, we've worried that several planets in the same empire might end up racing each other, and it wouldn't go well with our people who didn't choose the winner."

"It was all decided ahead of time," Yvella's mother told Kelly. "Bringing in tens of millions of Humans and making sure they have enough to eat is too expensive for most worlds to undertake just on speculation. Your people drive a hard bargain when they know that they're wanted. The planet administrator had to grant the businesses tax-free status for the next thousand years, or as long as the tunnel connection remains active without our signing the treaty and becoming members."

"Do you think you could sign the tunnel network treaty in the end after millions of years of avoiding it?"

"Given the advantages, yes. It's our business interests that kept us from ever signing the treaty in the past—some of the rules on warranty returns and sharing diagnostic codes are just more than they were willing to accept. But the mutual defense pact would save appreciable money, and the situation in our neighborhood is somewhat altered since the last time we refused membership."

Eighteen

"I'm too busy," Dorothy said, brandishing her tab. "If reconciling accounts and filling out safety sheets is how Shaina and Brinda used to spend most of their time, I can't blame them for taking indefinite leave to manage the *All Species Cookbook*. At least that comes with free food."

"You're the only one who can do it," Dietro said. "Even though it was my last chance to save the show, I never quite believed that Ofer's idea to have the Tharks identify contestants for us would work. But thirty-two of the first hundred prospects contacted by the Grenouthian casting department agreed to schedule an audition, and seven of them showed up at the network offices by way of reply."

"You mean, they hopped a space liner and came on the chance that the show eventually airs?"

"I think the invitations the casting department sent out implied it was a sure thing, but the point is, *Mage Search* has jumped to the top of the priority list for shows in development, and some of the network's top production personnel, from directors on down, are maneuvering to be part of it. You wouldn't believe some of the gifts I've been getting from bunnies I've never even met."

"You being showered with bribes and that means I have to drop everything and design mage apparel for the contestants?" Dorothy demanded. "I don't even know what it should look like."

"Ahem," Baa said, flourishing the loose sleeves of her silk robe that prevented the feathers on her arms from developing split ends while she kept them covered in the corridors. "You did design my casual wear."

"That was just a form-follows-function thing, and if I remember, you made Samuel ask me to design it for you because you didn't want to owe me a favor."

"Build on it," Dietro said. "For Baa, the loose sleeves were the key, but you made them look stylish."

"I copied the sleeves from a kimono I saw in a Gre-nouthian documentary about Geishas," Dorothy admitted. "And I only added the red hood because Baa specifically asked. I still think it looks weird."

"This is your chance to correct it. Here, give me your tab. I'll finish reconciling the spreadsheets and get the final report to Jeeves. You can take however long you need to come up with a thematic style for the mage robes on the show as long as you finish by next Friday."

"Next Friday? That's only eleven days!"

"I meant this Friday," Dietro said. "Humanese must be the only language in the galaxy where this means next and next means the one after."

"Surely you don't expect me to design a new line of fashion in four days," Dorothy said. "I'm not artificial intelligence, you know."

Dietro stopped trying to pull Dorothy's tab out of her death grip and stepped back like he'd received an electrical shock. "Affie's right—I am an idiot. How could I have missed it?"

"Missed what?"

"This is our biggest advertising opportunity ever. It's not just a product placement like Baa's Bags or our new line of Mystique Jewelry, this is a chance to put SBJ Fashions front and center of every broadcast of *Mage Search.*"

"For that kind of exposure, the Grenouthians will want a piece of the action," Baa said.

"For that kind of exposure, they can have it," Dietro said. "Let's see. I get five points as the creator, and I gave you twenty-five percent to be the magical consultant. The Grenouthians would normally ask for fifty percent on any sort of subsidiary rights deal, but I bet we can flip the script and give them points in the new line instead."

"Why subsidiary rights?" Dorothy asked, temporarily putting aside her show of dismay over being asked to provide the wardrobe for the multi-species cast auditions of a reality show on four days of notice. "The show was your idea."

"The Grenouthians have been at the forefront of the Stryxnet broadcast segment of the tunnel network entertainment business for millions of years, and that's the way they work. But we've got a robust enough accounting system to silo a new fashion line away from the rest of the business. They aren't going to settle for five points, but I bet we could get them for twenty."

"On the net profit," Baa said. "Leave it to a Grenouthian attorney to put twenty percent of the gross in a contract and try to slip it past you at the signing."

"Don't sign anything without Tzachan," Dorothy advised. "And ask Aisha for the name of her Thark agent who handles the periodic renegotiations of her contract."

"Does this mean you'll design something for me?" Jyndal asked shyly. "Ofer keeps saying that it's ridiculous that I work for a fashion design business and dress like a welder."

"Haven't you told him that those clothes are all for your protection?" Baa asked. "They're fireproof, arc-over proof, and plasma discharge resistant. That cloak I gave you would survive in a star's corona, which is more than I can say for your corporeal incarnation at this point of your development."

"Wait a second," Dietro said, looking at Dorothy suspiciously. "You switched from arguing that it's an impossible deadline to giving me negotiating advice in a hurry. What aren't you telling us?"

"It's possible that I started thinking about a new line of mage clothes for LARPing when you first had the idea for the show last year," Dorothy said with a cat-who-ate-the-canary smile. "It's possible I already designed thematically consistent robes for all of the species who participate in the Professional LARPing League, but I was holding off bringing it up until Myst's new jewelry line was established so I wouldn't steal her thunder."

"Let's see," Baa demanded, showing an eagerness that was rare for the seemingly ageless Terragram. "Do you have 3D renderings or are they on your artist's tab? I should have thought to check the tab earlier."

"It wouldn't have helped because I've been drawing them on paper with crayons. After that last incident with my cross-species golden-ratio designs getting stolen by hackers, I've been doing a lot of my work in Margie's art pads."

"Can we go to Mac's Bones and see them now?" Dietro asked.

"You don't have to," Dorothy said, going over to Affie's unused workbench and opening one of the large, flat drawers. "I brought in the one with the finished drawings and hid it where I knew nobody would ever look."

Baa, Dietro, and Jyndal crowded around as Dorothy slowly flipped the pages, pointing out some of the difficulties she'd had to overcome, like the sleeves from the upper arms of a Dollnick robe drooping down onto the lower arms, or the tentacle sheath at the base of the hood for the Drazen version.

"Shouldn't they have pointy hats with broad brims?" Dietro asked.

"Have you ever seen me in a pointy hat?" Baa demanded. "You're confusing mages with witches."

"Do they all come with fabric belts that have to be tied?" Jyndal asked. "I'm terrible at undoing knots that I've made."

"These are just the presentation robes," Dorothy said. "I also designed practical versions for LARPing, where loose clothing can be dangerous when you're trying to sneak through the woods, and I've been working on casual clothes that say 'mage' in an understated way by alluding to the other designs with color schemes and muted elements." She flipped forward to a drawing that looked like a standard Frunge business suit except for a certain droopiness in the sleeves and bagginess in the pant legs that gave the impression of a skirt.

"That works better than I might have guessed," Baa said grudgingly.

"Everybody associates black with magic, but it's just too gloomy, and I was worried that the cameras wouldn't like it. Eventually, I settled on grey with red highlights, but the presentation robes have a black lining, and they're reversible if you want to look foreboding."

"How close are you to patterns we can give our stitchers and get some samples made up for the auditions?" Dietro asked. "I have to say that the only one of the candidates the Tharks turned up who looks the part was wearing a sort of robe when she got here. Clothes make all the difference."

"What's everybody looking at?" Myst asked as she dropped her school bag at her design station. "Oh, are you finally showing them your mage designs, Dorothy? Did you tell them about the accessories?"

"Accessories?" the Vergallian sales manager asked in a hollow voice.

"You know, the bags and the jewelry. I've been thinking—"

"Hold that thought," Jeeves announced from the doorway. "I was remotely retuning the smoke alarms and I happened to catch the last few minutes of your conversation."

"Since when are there smoke alarms on Stryx stations?" Dorothy asked skeptically.

"Since Jyndal started working here. But the reason I was listening in is irrelevant. We need to have a meeting before this goes any farther, and I've pinged Flazint and Affie to come."

"What about Lancelot?"

"He's on his way," Myst said. "I think he was up all night with his stupid computers again, but he said he just needed a quick shower."

"If Shaina and Brinda are coming, we won't have room for everybody in the breakroom," Dorothy said.

"They delegated me to speak for them," the young Stryx said. "I have to take care of a few quick errands, but I hope to see you all sitting at the table with the stimulant of your choice in five minutes."

"That was odd," Dietro said after Jeeves zipped off.

"He seemed stressed about something," Jyndal said. "I hope he didn't get in trouble for my setting fire to the bulkhead."

"It's metal," Dorothy pointed out.

"Everything burns if you get it hot enough," Baa said. "And I put it out before it could do any real damage. I'll bet nobody even noticed after Jeeves patched the hole into the storeroom next door."

Flazint entered the design room, her droopy hair vines testifying that she'd been woken in the middle of the night. She sniffed and asked, "Who's been burning metal?"

"Me, and it was unintentional," Jyndal said. "We're having a meeting."

"I heard. I just stuck my head in to find out where everybody was."

By the time the office employees of SBJ Fashions gathered in the breakroom, almost ten minutes had passed, and Jeeves was uncharacteristically late. Dorothy found herself playing barista, fixing different alien teas for her friends, and finally coffee for herself, Baa, and Lancelot, who did look like he'd been up all night. Everybody ended up studying the crayon sketches of mage clothing, and the Japanese sleeves on the robes proved to be a hit. Jyndal even told Dietro that she was willing to go with him to model a robe for the Grenouthians, provided she got to keep it afterward.

"I'm sincerely sorry about being late," Jeeves said when he finally floated in. "I had to seek permission from my elders for something, and while that usually takes picoseconds, today it turned into a whole multiverse debate that, well, you saw how long it took."

"It takes me more time to get Richard to go to bed if he doesn't want to sleep," Dorothy said.

"Having already wasted several more minutes of everyone's time than I intended, I'll come quickly to the point. Shaina and Brinda won't be returning to the office."

"You fired them?"

"They retired," Jeeves said. "My former partners never cared about formal titles and job descriptions, which was very forward-thinking of them, but now that we're a growing concern with hundreds of full-time and part-time seamstresses working for us on the station, I think a little formality is called for. Congratulations Dietro and Dorothy on becoming the co-presidents of SBJ Fashions."

Affie shocked everybody by grabbing Dietro's face between her hands and kissing him right on the mouth. "You're writing up a proposal for my mother tonight," she said. "I'll help you with the forms."

"Could I be a vice president instead?" Dorothy asked. "It will look better for Dietro when he pitches Affie's mom, plus he's much more business oriented than I am."

"He's also busier than you are and looks on course to spend much of the next decade jumping through Vergallian courting hoops," Jeeves said.

"Have Shaina and Brinda retained their ownership share?" Baa asked.

"They've agreed on a price to sell it back to our treasury as cash flow allows. I hope that will incentivize you all to spend less and earn more so that the equity can be transferred on to you."

"But why would you need permission from your elders to reorganize SBJ Fashions?" Dorothy asked. "Do you owe them all money?"

"Our discussion was unrelated to Shaina and Brinda," Jeeves said.

"It was about my setting fire to the bulkhead, wasn't it?" Jyndal asked, her hands trembling with emotion. "Do I have to leave Union Station, or am I too dangerous to be allowed to wander around free?"

"Really, child," Baa said. "Geb, give the girl something to do with her hands."

A black cat suddenly became visible on the table, strutted over to Jyndal, and hopped down on her lap. Baa's apprentice automatically began stroking Geb's silky fur, and his purring immediately lowered everyone's stress levels to the point that Dorothy found herself nodding off.

"Without the area-of-effect spell, if you don't mind," Baa added, and the nodding heads around the table suddenly jerked awake.

"And indirectly, that's what my elders were on about," Jeeves said. "As you may remember from Baa's unwanted suitor, Stryx take a dim view of artificial means used to enslave the hearts and minds of sentients. It's bad enough that you're always falling in love with the wrong—but I digress. My elders will be watching with interest to see how Dietro's show impacts the acceptance of unexplained phenomena on the tunnel network, but a potential conflict of interest arose for me when you brainstormed the idea of launching a new line of fashion for mages."

"Are there really that many out there waiting to be discovered?" Dorothy asked.

"I assume the bulk of the buyers will be live-action role players and LARPing fans, but that's not the point. I can't be an active participant in the only business on the tunnel network that's promoting magic, because it gives the impression that the Stryx are expressing our support."

There was silence for a moment, and then Dietro said, "That's okay, the show will be fine without the business synergy. I'll keep my share private and pay Dorothy for her designs. There's no need to bring SBJ Fashions into it. We don't have to take advantage of every marketing opportunity that comes up."

"Actually, we do," Jeeves said. "Ignoring business opportunities is one thing, ignoring free advertising is the definition of insanity. That's why I'll be transferring my equity stake to the treasury and exiting with Shaina and Brinda."

"No," Dorothy said. "You can't just remove yourself from the business after all you've done for us. Besides, if you step back, Baa will eat the rest of us for lunch."

"I probably will," the Terragram mage concurred.

"A new line of mage clothes and accessories sounded cool, but we were just talking, and I don't have the time. It's going to be hard enough running the business after Shaina and Brinda exit—"

"A business you've been running for months now," Jeeves interjected.

"—without you dumping all the purchasing responsibilities in our laps. Are Dietro and I supposed to run off to the Chintoo orbital every other cycle to negotiate just-in-time manufacturing contracts with the artificial people for our shoes and jewelry? And we've never had to raise a cred for the business, it's all been you borrowing from your elders. Are you going to take yourself out of the business and continue functioning as our piggy bank? It doesn't make any sense."

"But it's free advertising," Jeeves protested. "That's the philosopher's stone of business."

"I thought that the philosopher's stone of business was spotting the next big trend in retail before it happens,"

Dorothy countered. "I remember reading that somewhere."

"Probably in your mother's notebook, because that's something the Thark ambassador told her about investing."

"Do you eavesdrop on all of my family's conversations?"

"How do you know I wasn't listening in on the Thark ambassador," Jeeves pointed out. "He's a funny guy."

Dietro stood up, looking very presidential. "We haven't even gone to the Grenouthians with the idea of cross holdings yet, and the more I think about it, the more complicated it becomes. They may not even like Dorothy's designs."

"Fat chance of that," Affie said.

"I agree with Dorothy. It would be dishonorable of us to let Jeeves throw himself on his sword just so we can enter a new niche market of uncertain value. I move we preemptively reject any offer from the Grenouthians to establish a direct relationship with SBJ Fashions in the matter of *Mage Search*."

"Second the motion," Affie said immediately.

"Third," Lancelot added, proving that he wasn't sleeping with his eyes open.

"The motion is carried," Dietro said, and he sat down looking rather pleased with himself.

"This is awkward," Jeeves remarked after a pause in which nobody else spoke. "As the Stryx expert on humanity, I told my elders that there was less than a one-in-ten chance of your changing your minds when I explained my position."

"I would have voted the same way if Affie and Lancelot hadn't beaten me to it," Dorothy said. "But I still have a question. How come this problem of magical appearances didn't come up already with Baa's Bags?"

"It did," Jeeves said. "But everybody understands that Terragram mages are unique and that I was doing a public service by getting Baa involved in gainful employment."

"And my jewelry for the Live Action Role Playing broadcasts?" Myst asked.

"Stryx librarians handle the infrastructure for the professional LARPing league," Jeeves explained. "It's not seen as SBJ Fashions taking a stand on the flavor or existence of magic."

"But you employ me as a mage's apprentice," Jyndal said.

"An apprentice works for a master by definition, and that's Baa. If I started hiring winners from Dietro's show to do enchantments for Baa's Bags, that might put me back over the line."

"Find out," Baa suggested. "I was thinking that *Mage Search* wouldn't be a bad way to recruit talent, and I was going to suggest to the Grenouthians that becoming one of my apprentices could be a prize for winning the show."

"I'm not sure I understand why your elders care if the tunnel network species see the Stryx as taking a stand on magic," Affie said slowly. "We all know that there are phenomena we can't explain. The stuff that isn't amenable to our current level of scientific analysis gets lumped into the magic category."

"I'd love to stick around and answer your question, but there's a ship departing for Earth with the ambassadors on board and I should be on it as well," Jeeves said. "Being the Stryx expert on humanity has its drawbacks, and accompanying the Historical Commission on their tour of Earth is one of them. Coming, Affie?"

"Methan is going, so I'm off the hook," the Vergallian said. "And with his daughter gone, I'll need to keep an eye on the experimental daycare."

Nineteen

"The fact that your people haven't already turned Atlantis into a major tourist attraction just shows you lack the technical and organizational know-how," the Grenouthian ambassador said, as he investigated the sub-standard buffet set out on the bridge of the chartered tourist ship. "I can ping a few theme park experts when we get back to President McAllister's office and they'll have a new historical preserve up and running by the end of the year. Or should I say, down and running, since it's underwater."

"I've told you three times already that we didn't know Atlantis was here," Daniel said, frowning at a cellophane package of something orange that claimed to be peanut butter and crackers. "Sure, there were always rumors about a sunken island civilization, but we didn't have the technology to detect stone buildings buried so deep below sediment and volcanic ash, not to mention the ocean."

"Or we could just raise the whole thing for you," the Dollnick ambassador offered. "It might take a century or two, given all of the underwater mining required, but any of our terraforming engineers could manage it with three hands tied behind their backs." He let out a sad whistle. "Isn't there any fresh produce?"

"We aren't here to eat or to discover new tourist attractions," the Verlock ambassador said sternly. "Atlantis can stay where it is until the Humans develop the necessary technology to discover it on their own."

"Are we assuming that the inhabitants were Humans?" Ambassador Bork asked as he cut through the thick red wax on a small round of cheese that may have been aging for a century. Once he saw the inside, the iron-stomached Drazen left it on the platter. "The doorways were higher and narrower than anything else I've seen on Earth, and the chairs in the throne room were for a species with longer legs than either Humans or Alts."

"That's the problem with these non-invasive archeological tours," the Frunge ambassador said. He lifted the wine goblet he'd just filled from a box labeled 'Red' and examined it against the light streaming through the thick porthole glass as the ship sliced through the atmosphere at hypersonic speeds. "If this were an excavation, we could have cleaned off some of those mosaics and no doubt found artistic representations of the inhabitants. Instead, we traveled to the bottom of the ocean just to wander among holographic renderings created by a dozen subterranean imaging techniques." He set the goblet back down on the table and added, "Speaking of sediment…"

"There's some chocolate spread here, Gwendolyn," Daniel called to the Gem ambassador who'd been hanging back from the usual food scrum. "What did you think of Atlantis?"

"It's sad to imagine a whole civilization lost beneath the waves," the clone said, coming forward to examine the plastic tub. After reading the ingredients, she left it unopened. "But if rumors about Atlantis were preserved in Human arts and literature, it means that the cultures existed side-by-side, or in close temporal proximity. Kelly told me that Humans had completely forgotten about the existence of the Alts until the discovery of cave paintings and other artifacts tens of thousands of years after the Stryx removed the survivors from the planet. I wonder, though. Could the Atlantis civilization have been Alts who didn't make the trip?"

"Our traditional songs stretch back to our exile from Earth and there's nothing in them about members of our race staying behind," Methan contributed.

"You're the Human expert," Ambassador Aleeytis addressed Jeeves. "Did the Atlantis civilization consist of Humans, or was it a Neanderthal population that was left behind?"

"I'm younger than any of you here, including Daniel," Jeeves said. "How would I know?"

"Do you expect me to answer that?"

"I wouldn't tell you anyway because it would spoil all of the fun. It's bad enough that I got drafted into playing tour guide for a Historical Commission site visit. I'm not going to make it worse by doing your homework for you."

"What's with the food, Jeeves?" the Vergallian followed up. "The only thing here I would consider eating is the vegan squeeze tube emergency ration, but I'll have to get a lot hungrier first. Are you trying to make some sort of point?"

"The caterer came recommended," Jeeves said. "I can't imagine what went wrong."

"While we're on the subject of not doing one's homework, did you all read the package I prepared?" Srythlan asked.

"I tried," Daniel said. "I don't know how the page numbers on my tab would correspond with a printed book, but I made it to a thousand and something."

"May I assume that our colleague from EarthCent got farther than the rest of you?" the Verlock inquired after giving up on finding anything worth tasting at the buffet.

"We all know how much you like explaining history, Srythlan, so we wanted to save reading the package as a review for after you give us the lecture," the Grenouthian ambassador said.

Srythlan shuffled over to the seating area where the Chert was chugging a bottle of Union Station Springs water he'd brought along, which the other ambassadors were eyeing like hungry jackals. "Our next stop is the Chicxulub crater," the Verlock continued at his best public speaking cadence. "It is one of the largest impact craters on Earth, the only one with an easily viewed peak ring, and further evidence of the impact is given by the presence of shocked quartz and tektites."

"If it's really big, I would expect a gravity anomaly," Ambassador Crute said.

"Spoken like a true Dollnick. Yes, there is a gravity anomaly as well. But the main point of interest for us is that the dating of the crater coincides with a mass extinction event on Earth some sixty-six million years ago. It put an end to the dominant reptilian species, dinosaurs, and thereby allowed for the eventual rise of Humans and Alts."

"That's a lot of assumptions," the Fillinduck ambassador said. "I was under the impression that neither Humans nor Alts have existed for a million years in their current forms. What were they doing with the other sixty-five million years?"

"Hiding in trees from predators," the Grenouthian ambassador said. "A distant relative of mine produced an excellent documentary on the subject."

"So you're telling me that the Humans located an impact crater and connected it with an extinction event?" Ptew asked. "I can think of a dozen other possibilities, including volcanic activity or alien invasion."

"In this instance, the existence of the impact crater was predicted from the other side of the ocean based on the discovery of a thin layer of clay in the geological record that included high levels of iridium," Srythlan said. Then he waited patiently like a schoolteacher trying to encourage class participation

"Iridium is rare on planets, common in asteroids," the Frunge ambassador said dutifully. "I remember that from Mining 101."

"Ambassador Ptew raised an interesting point," Daniel said. "I don't want to make it sound like everything needs to be about us, but it seems a bit far-fetched to point at a disaster from sixty-six million years ago and say that it was critical in the eventual appearance of primates. I did read through your discussion on population bottlenecks and the limited geographical range of early hominids, and it left me with the impression that humanity must have narrowly escaped extinction dozens of times just in the last few hundred thousand years."

"And if you had read far enough to get to the Chicxulub crater, you would have learned that we aren't visiting it for possible inclusion as a Human historical site," Srythlan said.

"Are you saying that Earth produced another technological species that made it off the planet?" the Grenouthian ambassador demanded. "Sixty-six million years ago predates the rise of our species by an order of magnitude, and other than the Stryx, I'm not aware of any extant life-form that keeps records that far back. But now that you mention it, some of those fossilized dinosaurs from the documentary bore a resemblance to the dragon variants that have evolved on so many worlds."

"Surely we would have found archeological evidence by this time," Daniel said. "A race of space-faring dinosaurs would have left behind obvious traces."

"After sixty-six million years?" Srythlan countered. "Your people consider Atlantis a legend, and that sank beneath the sea less than ten thousand years ago."

"But the smart dinosaurs would have been all over the planet, not just on an island."

"You can't assume that an advanced species of dinosaurs would act or think anything like Humans," the Dollnick ambassador cautioned Daniel. "Perhaps their evolution was fast-tracked, and they were focused on the stars from the start of their technological development. Not every species remains fixated on killing each other and everything else they see as a threat for as long as Humans did. Another civilization may have risen and evacuated Earth before the asteroid hit."

"But dinosaur fossils are as common as rocks in some places," Daniel pointed out.

"Dinosaurs roamed the Earth for over a hundred million years," Srythlan told him. "Given the numbers that lived during that period, it would be unimaginable if some examples hadn't died in circumstances that allowed their fossilized remains to survive to this day."

"And there's the Neatness Hypothesis," the Vergallian ambassador said, looking thoughtful. "There was an exercise in my royal training where we were asked to plan the evacuation of a planet without leaving any trace of our civilization behind. I remember that the hardest part was getting rid of stone artifacts and large earthen features, such as mounds."

"Nature has a way of erasing large engineering projects if they aren't maintained," Crute said. "It depends on the planet, of course, and artifacts can last a long time in deserts or certain burial conditions. But deserts themselves come and go as long as a planet remains geologically active."

"I get that bridges and skyscrapers will fall down, but what about the Greek ruins we toured yesterday?" Daniel asked.

"Mere thousands of years old, and clearly restored," Srythlan told him. "Do you think those columns survived standing this long in an earthquake zone?"

"So what are we going to see at this impact crater?" the Horten ambassador groused, sounding rather cross over not having found anything to eat. "If we wanted to look at craters, the oversized moon up there is so pockmarked with them that they're on top of each other."

"Didn't the asteroid vaporize on contact?" the Grenouthian asked.

"That's the theory," Srythlan said. "But the important thing is—"

"Eating," the Drazen ambassador interrupted. "What's the point of going to look at the sights if all we can think about is food?"

"I've made a note of your disappointment with my catering arrangements, but I don't see what I can do about it now," Jeeves said. "When we get back to the spaceport, I'll buy you all a meal."

"Or we could skip the sixty-six-million-year-old hole in the seafloor and get back to the New World's Fair, where we could be learning about Human cultures from all around the world by sampling their food," Bork said.

"Second the motion," Czeros and the Grenouthian ambassador said simultaneously.

"Third," Aleeytis added a split second later.

"As chair of the Historical Commission, I must insist on a full vote for the record to change the itinerary set out by the Stryx," Srythlan said. "All in favor?"

Daniel felt his arm being pulled up, and glancing over, saw Bork's tentacle wrapped around the wrist. "I was voting with you anyway," he said.

"Just making sure," the Drazen ambassador said. "Jeeves?"

"I don't have a vote, but I do have a veto. In this instance, the list of sites to visit was drawn up by my elders to get your support for nominating Earth as—"

"I nominate Earth for whatever," Ortha interrupted.

"Second the motion," Crute said.

"Third," the Chert ambassador added. "Can we go get something to eat now?"

"I'll need an official vote for the record," Jeeves said.

Srythlan let out a sad sigh. "All in favor of skipping Chicxulub and nominating Earth as an advanced prospect for the Tunnel Network Historical Attractions and postponing its consideration as a Galactic Historical Site until further notice?"

All of the hands shot up, and then the ambassadors shifted their balance to compensate as the ship began a wide turn towards the north. "Estimated arrival in forty minutes," Jeeves said. "I've sent a text to Acting President McAllister informing her of our change in plans."

"Joe knows all of the good barbeque places," Bork said, elbowing Czeros.

The party of ambassadors stayed together long enough to take the monorail from the ship's parking spot to the New World's Fair, but they broke apart into groups with similar food interests as soon as Acting President McAllister and her special assistant ushered them through the gate for free entrance.

"How did it go?" Kelly asked Daniel.

"Disaster," the associate ambassador reported. "A couple of days of complaining about the catering, topped by the ambassadors all voting to postpone making Earth a Galactic Historical Site until the Stryx bring it up again. I don't know if it would have been a good thing or a bad thing, but I wish they'd put a little more consideration into the matter before making up their minds. It seems disrespectful to decide the fate of our planet based on the quality of some contract caterers that we didn't even have a say in picking."

"Who did?"

"Jeeves. I thought that as the senior human on the trip, I'd be responsible for sorting out all the details, but a couple of weeks ago, he told me that as the Stryx expert on humanity, he could take it off my plate. The thing I don't understand is how he could have screwed it up so—" Daniel stopped abruptly and stared at Kelly. "He couldn't have, could he?"

"The ambassadors aren't exactly picky eaters, and one of the few services I've utilized on Earth that's not badly lagging the equivalent on Union Station is the catering," Kelly said as she led them in the general direction of the Human Empire pavilion. "It sounds to me like Jeeves has been up to his usual tricks."

"But what does he have to gain by getting the ambassadors to break off the site inspection before looking at a giant underwater impact crater from over sixty million years ago? And if that was the goal all along, why would the Stryx have added Earth to the consideration list for Galactic Historical Sites?"

"I don't imagine it was to give all the ambassadors a free junket to visit the New World's Fair. Aabina?"

"Maybe there was something that Jeeves wanted everybody to see, and after that, it was just a waste of his time," the Vergallian suggested. "What was your last stop before the Chicxulub crater?"

"Atlantis," Daniel replied. "Ambassador Crute said that the Dollnicks could raise it for us, and the Grenouthian ambassador suggested that they could turn it into a theme park, though I don't know where he planned to find Atlantean reenactors when we don't know anything about them."

"Did you get the impression that Jeeves wanted us to do something about this now?" Kelly asked. "Was the site in danger from, I don't know, underwater volcanic activity or something?"

"It was already buried. We didn't even see the actual buildings, just a holographic reconstruction that could have been faked as easily—" Daniel interrupted himself for the second time in just a couple of minutes. "What if the Atlantis we saw wasn't real at all? Jeeves said that the ship was imaging buried buildings from its sensor array, but he could have been feeding it data from anywhere."

"I notice he didn't accompany you back to the fair."

"He had business and took off in a different direction."

"Were any of the other sites visited out of the ordinary?" Aabina asked. "Places that aren't already widely known to Earth's archaeologists?"

"Atlantis is the only one that fits that category," Daniel said. "One of the ambassadors brought up that we have no way of knowing whether it was even a human site, and somebody suggested that it could have been an Alt community that remained on Earth after the Stryx evacuated the rest of them. Methan said there was no record of that in their legends, but maybe Jeeves was hinting that Atlantis was protected from humans by the Stryx."

"After tens of thousands of years, they suddenly let the remaining Alts all drown?" Kelly asked. "That doesn't sound right to me."

"Earth isn't a Stryx station," Affie pointed out. "There's no reason to believe that they're monitoring what goes on around the clock. I can imagine a situation where they'd do something to give Alts who refused to move away a chance at surviving by moving them to an isolated continent and then leaving them to their own devices."

"We might not be able to model the tectonic activity of a planet for tens of thousands of years into the future, but I'll bet it's child's play for the Stryx."

"Maybe that was the whole point," Daniel said suddenly. "Jeeves might have been delegated to deliver the message that Earth being a Stryx protectorate doesn't mean that they're going to hold our hands and keep us safe forever." He stopped when he realized they were standing outside the Human Empire's pavilion. "So that's what it looks like up close. Samuel was right. It's pretty impressive for a tent."

"We aren't going to solve this by debating the point, but see if you can get a read as to what went on from the other ambassadors," Kelly suggested. "President Beyer's sabbatical is winding down, and I was looking forward to pulling a disappearing act, but now I'll have to meet him and explain what happened. Maybe he'll have a better idea of what it might mean since he lives here."

Twenty

"Welcome back, Ambassador," Judith greeted Kelly when the latter strolled into the embassy at half past ten on Monday morning. "The Director of EarthCent Intelligence stopped in to see you earlier, but after talking to Ofer, he went back to his office and asked me to ping him when you arrived."

"Clive must have forgotten that I'd be transitioning to part-time on my return," Kelly said, trying to figure out what had changed about the embassy in her absence. "Did you move your display desk closer to the wall?"

"It's a hologram," the new embassy manager said. "Libby, could you drop the privacy screen?"

The reception area was suddenly restored to its original size. The floor space that had been concealed was revealed to show an improvised nursery, complete with mats, two bouncy seats, one of the largest collections of building blocks the ambassador had ever seen, and a low-slung tricycle. A baby that might have been nearing its first birthday was lying on its back on a padded mat while a sibling of perhaps three was pretending to read a story from a toy tab.

"Doesn't it make you nervous to know that the children could be up to anything without you seeing, even though they're right behind you?" Kelly asked.

"Do you think I'm wearing these glasses because I'm one of those luddites who won't get their eyes fixed?" Judith replied with a laugh. "They neutralize standard holograms, and the funny thing is that I never knew how many active holograms there were on Union Station until I forgot I was wearing the glasses and went shopping after work."

"I've learned to be suspicious of large potted plants. The Hortens sell an inexpensive privacy hologram that covers just enough area for a seated humanoid."

The consul came out of his office reading something on his tab, and said, "I'll be in the conference room, Judith," before his peripheral vision made him look up and notice Kelly. "Ambassador McAllister. Welcome back. Is this going to be your new starting time?"

"I haven't planned that far ahead," Kelly admitted. "The new guidelines for ambassadors over sixty-five with a minimum of thirty years in grade is twenty-five hours a week, but it's up to me whether to come in three days a week, five hours a day, or whatever else makes the math work."

"Could you work fifty hours a week every other week?"

"If I was your age I could. I'm cutting back because I don't have the energy I did ten years ago and it's not fair to everyone who comes to see me. I won't be surprised if I can get more done in a five-hour day than an eight-hour day."

"Efficiency," Judith said, nodding her head. "When I was working at the EarthCent Intelligence training camp, I realized that by the end of the day, most of the trainees were just going through the motions. It's a way to build mental toughness, but exhausted people do poorly at learning new things. Thomas always scheduled the challenging activities for the morning."

"Have you pinged Director Oxford to tell him that Ambassador McAllister is back?" Ofer asked Judith. "He said it was very important."

"It's Kelly, that goes for both of you, and if you want me to know who you're talking about, Director Oxford is Clive," the EarthCent ambassador said. "Yes, please tell him I'm here and that I'll be in my office. Were you on your way to a meeting, Ofer?"

"Daniel is waiting for me," Ofer said, glancing over his shoulder at the door to the conference room shared between the EarthCent Embassy and CoSHC's offices. "He must be wondering what happened."

"Go ahead, and I'll let you both know when Clive gets here if he's willing to talk to the three of us at the same time," Kelly said. She smiled at the three-year-old who had stopped pretending to read and was staring at her with trepidation. "I can see it's going to take a while to win your children's trust," she added to Judith.

"She's only here today because the Alt daycare is closed for one of their holidays," the embassy manager said. "Their contract queen talked me into starting Katie there last month, and she really enjoys it. Robbie still sleeps most of the time so he's not a fun companion for a three-year-old."

"Dorothy said that her son likes the Alt daycare so much that he cries when she goes to take him home," Kelly said. "The best part of being a grandparent is seeing the chickens come home to roost."

"Excuse me?"

"Wait another thirty years and you'll know what I mean."

When Kelly put her purse in the deep drawer of her display desk, it struck her that the six months she'd spent on Earth covering for President Beyer had flown by in what felt like just a few weeks. Before closing the drawer, she retrieved her paperback notebook from the purse and began flipping through the pages from the back to see if there was anything urgent she'd forgotten. Suddenly she looked up at the ceiling and asked, "Are the Stryx using humanity as a loss leader, Libby?"

"You'll have to give me a little more context," the Stryx librarian replied.

"You know what I mean. I've been wondering about it ever since you opened the tunnel to Onkle Four for the Sharf. I think that you're trying to get more species to join the tunnel network by letting them slide on the treaty obligations and using us as the excuse."

"Are you worried that would cheapen your species in some way?"

"Not cheapen, exactly, but if the other species get used to thinking of humans as something to stock up on because there's a bonus if you—maybe loss leader wasn't the best analogy," Kelly corrected herself. "How about trading stamps?"

"Everybody likes a bargain, even artificial intelligences," Libby said. "As to Onkle Four, it's not the first exception we've made for the Sharf."

"Do you mean Ada's recycling orbital? I haven't talked to her in decades, but now that you mention it, they did have a tunnel network connection, or I couldn't have ended up there. But I thought that was a special deal because the Sharf contracted to recycle all the derelict ships and lost containers from tunnel network shipping lanes."

"Do you think that a Dollnick prince wouldn't have bid on the work if we'd offered, or a Frunge? They have more ore processing facilities than the Sharf, and metal recycling in space is low-hanging fruit for them."

"But orbitals aren't anywhere near as populated as planets, and they're often located in star systems where there aren't any inhabited worlds," Kelly said, nodding her head. "Now that I think of it, aren't there tunnel network connections to some other orbitals belonging to species that never signed the treaty?"

"It's worth it to keep the door open to dialogue, and it's not the economic boon to the orbital owners that you might think," Libby said. "Since none of the host species have tunnel networks of their own, it means their only access to the connection we give the orbital is by jump ships."

"And if they need a jump ship to get to the orbital, they may as well jump wherever they're going and skip the tunnel, unless there's a big cost difference. How do the tunnel tolls compare to the wear-and-tear on a jump drive?"

"That's competitive business information, but I'm sure any of the ambassadors would fill you in on the economics if you asked."

"So let me see if I have this straight," Kelly said, her pencil poised over a blank page in her notebook. "At some point in the past, you started offering connections to orbitals for species you were trying to interest in tunnel network membership, but it didn't do the trick. Then we came along, and you thought, why not offer a connection to any human community over twenty million? A non-tunnel-network-species like the Sharf thinks they're taking advantage of a loophole to get a connection, but in reality, you want to get a whole star system hooked on the advantages so they'll reconsider signing the treaty."

"Clive is here," the Stryx librarian announced. A second later, Kelly's door slid open, and the director of EarthCent Intelligence entered.

"Welcome back, Ambassador," he said, extending the streak of friends and family who had greeted Kelly formally since her return. "Getting used to living in a giant spinning can again?"

"If you're talking about the gravity, I can't tell the difference, and when I saw our beat-up ice harvester in Mac's Bones, I knew I was home," Kelly said. "We're going to invite everybody for a picnic Saturday. Joe is busy restocking the pantry after the kids ran everything down when we were gone."

"I stuck my head in the conference room on the way here and invited Daniel and Ofer to join us as soon as they submit the forms. It shouldn't be more than a couple minutes."

"What forms? If you tell me they're applying for jobs somewhere else, I'm going home."

"Nothing like that," Clive said, making himself comfortable in his customary chair directly across the display desk from Kelly. "It turns out that commission work involves more paperwork, to use an archaic term, than sitting on a committee. Daniel is finishing up a report about his site inspection on Earth for the Historical Commission, and he's hoping that Ofer can fill out most of the forms for the Gambling Commission."

"As long as we're on the subject of paperwork, I brought you this," Kelly said, producing a paperback novel featuring a heavily tattooed Horten with bulging pectorals that looked like a Huktra's flight muscles.

"Thank you," Clive said, immediately recognizing the cover from the popular Pirate's Bride series that his wife published in translation. "I take it this is one of your notebooks and not a steamy romance?"

"How do you know that my notes aren't steamy?"

"Because you've shown them to me before and they're mainly reminders to yourself or advice you've received from aliens." He opened to the first page and read, "Ladies in Waiting, Georgia's mother, Queen Asiedu impressed."

"Exactly," Kelly said. "It's all of my notes about the alien diplomats and business delegations that Joe and I showed around the New World's Fair. I was surprised by how unguarded they were in their reactions to what they saw. It was almost like we were all taking a vacation from diplomacy."

"Interesting, but what does it mean?" Clive asked. "We've been getting reports about the Ladies in Waiting for a couple of years now, and the Galactic Free Press covers them in some depth. I assume the Georgia you're referring to is the wife of Larry, the Human Empire's Minister of Trade, but what does her mother have to do with the reigning head of the Council of Queens?"

"Oh, I guess I could have included a few more details. Janice was participating in public debates about the future of the Ladies in Waiting movement, and she impressed Queen Asiedu enough that they had a private meeting."

"Larry's mother-in-law met with the leader of the Empire of a Hundred Worlds? What did they talk about?"

Kelly shrugged. "I wasn't there, and Janice told us it was private Ladies in Waiting business. They could be plotting together to take over Earth for all I know."

"And you didn't think it was worth mentioning in our monthly holoconference call?"

"I thought I did. You know how my memory has been lately. And I'll need the notebook back after you make a copy."

"Any other bombshells?" Clive asked, flipping through the cryptic notes. "You know, I'm going to have to sit down with you and go through these one by one to make much sense of them."

"That's fine. I have plenty of time now that I've reduced my hours."

"But it's work. Doing this in your free time would defeat the whole purpose."

"Would it?" Kelly asked. "I love my job, you know. I just don't have the energy I once did, and I feel like I'd be cheating everybody if I just came in and punched the clock."

"Cayl luggage?" Clive read from the notebook. "I didn't know they sent a delegation to the New World's Fair. Did their luggage get lost?"

"Emperor Brynt's granddaughter came down when Flower stopped at Earth, but the note isn't about her. It's funny how many grandchildren of emperors I've met in the last six months."

"The luggage?"

"Right. There was a custom leatherworker at the fair making all sorts of saddlebags, and I ordered some for our Cayl hounds as a present. They like to come and help when we go shopping, but all we have for them are some lightweight Frunge bags that probably hold more weight but look cheap."

"So it's not all interspecies diplomacy," Clive said, flipping a few more pages. "You took all of them to the Human Empire pavilion to try out the virtual reality visors and meet Samuel?"

"I think that was why most of them came in the end," Kelly said with a self-deprecating laugh. "The famous EarthCent ambassador meeting the future rulers of the tunnel network empires and passing the diplomatic torch to her son at the Human Empire. None of them wasted any time trying to negotiate anything with me."

"Sorry we took so long," Daniel said as he entered Kelly's office with Ofer on his heels. "The site inspection report turned into an exercise in creative writing. If it had been the tunnel network ambassadors pushing me to cut corners as usual, I wouldn't have gone along with it, but since Jeeves was there, I have to assume that the Stryx approved."

"Approved of what?" Clive asked.

"We were supposed to inspect the crater where a giant asteroid put an end to the dinosaurs, but Jeeves manipulated everybody into agreeing to sign off without visiting."

"Why would he do that? The Stryx are the ones who set the agenda for those site inspections. If they didn't want the ambassadors going there, they could have left it off the list."

Daniel shrugged. "I just know that Jeeves intentionally screwed up the catering to give the ambassadors an excuse to cut the trip short. Everybody played along, but as much as they like food, I know that none of the aliens would let a missed meal or two get in the way of their duty. After I had time to sleep on it, I realized they were acting out a play for my benefit."

"What about the other commission you mentioned?" Kelly asked him.

"Samuel and his staff are going to have to do some hard thinking about how far they want to push the Human Lottery idea. Ofer can tell you about the details."

"My daughter told me that you were able to help Dietro finalize his show with the Grenouthians," Kelly said to the consul. "Something about the Thark ambassador helping out?"

"I was just the messenger, and I did it for Jyndal, not Dietro," Ofer replied. "I don't understand how it's not an ethical violation for tunnel network ambassadors to mix their public and private affairs, but you and Daniel have told me that they all do it, so I try to keep my mouth shut."

"None of it is happening without the Stryx knowing exactly what's going on," Clive reminded him. "Which brings me to the reason I'm here. EarthCent Intelligence has been tracking an exodus of workers at the end of their contracts leaving the tunnel network and not returning. One of our analysts looked at the data from the big contract worker job fair last year and tried to follow up to see whether it was worth repeating. Over five million people who were actively seeking work can no longer be located."

"Five million!" Kelly did a little quick math. "That's a thousand groups of five thousand. How can that many people just slip away?"

"Keeping in mind that roughly five billion people are involved in the contract work economy at any time if you include dependents, five million is only a tenth of a percent. And we're assuming that they left the tunnel network, because if they had taken new contracts, the data would have shown it. All the other species cooperated with our study because they're anxious for us to run another job fair."

"Considering that they hijacked the job fair we intended for CoSHC to recruit ex-contract workers for open worlds, it's not surprising," Daniel said sourly. "Did you attempt to follow up with family members, known acquaintances, that sort of thing?"

"The best data we have is from Vivian's GenePost app," Clive said, unable to hide a note of pride in his daughter's pet project for the Human Empire. "But once anybody leaves the tunnel network and loses access to the Stryxnet, the only communications are by cargo ship, since that's what mail essentially is—cargo. So we know that there's an outward flow of a minimum of five million people, but we don't know if they all went to the same place."

"And you think another species is stocking up on humans to make the twenty-million mark and get a tunnel network connection like the Sharf," Kelly surmised. "I don't like the idea of losing track of that many people, but assuming you're right, they must have been given a good deal."

"What if the aliens lied to them?" Ofer asked. "Like Director Oxford said, if they're off the tunnel network, they can't communicate unless they have access to interstellar ships."

"But the second part of the equation is earning a tunnel connection, and the Stryx aren't going to give another species one for holding twenty-million people captive."

"You don't think the Cayl..." Daniel began, and then shook his head. "No, their jump ships are among the best in the galaxy, and even with a tunnel, their empire is too far for quick transits. The Stryx would slow the traffic down to where it would take weeks."

"We're only aware of the species who happen to have had interactions with the tunnel network in the last century," Clive said. "There must be tens of thousands of spacefaring species in the galaxy we've never even heard of, if for no other reason than because it simply hasn't come up."

"All right," Kelly said. "You've given me something new to worry about. I promised President Beyer I'd submit a report as soon as I got back to the embassy, so why don't we all see what progress we can make on this puzzle and meet in the conference room on Friday morning."

"Eight A.M.?" Clive asked.

Kelly grimaced. "Let's make it ten."

After the men left, the EarthCent ambassador stuck her head out the office door, told Judith that she was busy for the next fifteen minutes if anybody came looking for her, and then engaged the security lock before returning to her desk. Just when she was about to ask Libby to start recording her report, the thing that had been gnawing at the back of her mind as out of place finally clicked, and she removed a shoe and threw it at the potted plant in the corner. As she expected, rather than knocking leaves off the fig tree, the shoe was caught by a pincer as the hologram dropped and Jeeves appeared.

"I believe you lost this," the young Stryx said, floating over to return her shoe.

"Really, Jeeves. I thought you had more sophisticated methods of eavesdropping than sneaking into a room and disguising yourself with a hologram. What did you do with my real Ficus?"

"I moved it to Ofer's office. He seemed in need of someone to talk to."

"I don't suppose you're going to volunteer the mystery destination of millions of humans."

"That would be confidential business information, but I can assure you they aren't being farmed as livestock, or any of the other nauseating uses for sentients that your science fiction writers are so fond of."

"Then why are you really here?" Kelly asked.

"Did Dorothy tell you that she objected to my retiring from SBJ Fashions?" Jeeves countered.

"The way I heard it, Dietro and the others beat her to the punch."

"But Dorothy is the one who would have been most affected. I have a deal to offer you."

"Put it in writing," Kelly said.

"It's not that kind of deal," Jeeves said, and the very air in the office began to hum with some sort of advanced anti-eavesdropping technology. "You hang on as ambassador until the Human Empire launches and I'll make sure that Dorothy doesn't waste her best years of motherhood arguing about micro-creds with suppliers."

Kelly sighed. "I appreciate the offer, but I'm confident you won't interfere with Dorothy's happiness in either case, and I don't know how much longer I can do this, even with reduced hours. When EarthCent set the retirement age for ambassadors to seventy-five, it was a mistake."

"Hypothetically speaking, I'd be surprised if you had to wait that long."

"I might manage to keep it together until I'm seventy-two if you can get my supplements refilled," Kelly said slyly. "I'm almost out of gingko and ginseng."

"You've dropped the fish oil?" Jeeves asked. "According to M793qK, that's the one that might actually help."

"How did you—should I take that as a yes?"

"I'll deliver the goods if you'll start working your way through the math puzzles."

"You drive a hard bargain," Kelly said. "Is there anything else?"

"There's always something else," Jeeves said. "That's what makes existence interesting."

From the Author

The next EarthCent release will be the third book in the **EarthCent Metaverse** series. If you're new to the EarthCent books, you can start back at the beginning with **Union Station 1, 2, 3**, a discounted three-book bundle.

For notifications of new releases, sign up for the mailing list at www.ifitbreaks.com. You may have noticed that Amazon notifications of new releases have become random, they missed three of my books in 2022. I also post new releases to facebook.com/E.M.Foner/ and respond to all temperate e-mail sent to e_foner@yahoo.com

Readers have asked me to include the complete timeline of the EarthCent Universe in order so here it is:

Destiny: Union Station
Date Night on Union Station
Alien Night on Union Station
High Priest on Union Station
Spy Night on Union Station
Carnival on Union Station
Wanderers on Union Station
Vacation on Union Station
Guest Night on Union Station
Word Night on Union Station
Party Night on Union Station
Review Night on Union Station
Family Night on Union Station
Book Night on Union Station
LARP Night on Union Station
Career Night on Union Station
Last Night on Union Station

Independent Living
Soup Night on Union Station
Assisted Living
Freelance on the Galactic Tunnel Network
Con Living
Empire Night on Union Station
Space Living
Traders on the Galactic Tunnel Network
Orphans on the Galactic Tunnel Network
Swap Night on Union Station
Slow Living
Artists on the Galactic Tunnel Network
History Night on Union Station
Bits of Anarchy
Double Living
Bits of Flower
Synergy on the Galactic Tunnel Network

Made in the USA
Middletown, DE
14 July 2023